SPEAKING TO THE DEAD WITH RADIOS

RADIO SWEEP ELECTRONIC VOICE PHENOMENA

By Michael Hobert Edwards

Michael Hobert Edwards

ISBN-13: 978-1479325955

Dedications:

I dedicate this book to four very important people in my life, first to my lovely wife Dini, second to my mother Martha Edwards, third to my deceased father Hobert Collin Edwards, and fourth to my neighbor, coach, and good friend the late John Don Cates.

If not for my lovely wife Dini Casas Edwards, who has supported me one hundred percent in my quest and interest in the paranormal, I would not have been able to engage and experience what I have thus far.

It was my mother Martha Edwards who taught me by example to help others, and through my life long experience with her watching her do good deeds for others all the while working as a nurse and an elementary school teacher, I too have taken her path but from a much different perspective. I help families connect with their deceased loved ones recording messages from them in the form of Electronic Voice Phenomena, paranormal messages that help the families know their loved ones are at peace in the spirit world. I have even taught others how to record directly with their families in the privacy of their homes. I dedicate this book in part to my mother, who by her own example helped me establish a path in helping others.

My father Hobert Collin Edwards who passed away in his sleep November 1987 due to natural causes, is largely responsible for me having written this book in the first place, and for my ever having gotten involved with the paranormal recording voices from the dead. I wanted to make contact with him, and by chance, which you will soon learn in reading this book, I finally did learn how to make contact with my father, and still communicate with him on a regular basis having amassed over five thousand recorded audio files of recorded electronic voice phenomena messages from him starting October 2008 to present day January 2012. If not for my quest to try and make contact with my father, you would not be reading this book.

John Don Cates was my neighbor, basketball coach, and as I moved into adulthood he became my friend, someone whom I could talk to about any subject, any time. As Mr. Cates three sons will tell you, their dad was always available to them, and he was always available to me. Don was there for me as a father figure when needed, and he never turned me away. Mr. Cates taught me by example to help others no matter how tired you are, and it is through my experiences with Don that I turn no one away that has come to me for help.

Just before John Don Cates passed away from cancer in 1994, I wrote this poem for him which he was able to enjoy!

<u>Going Home</u>

While I wait at Concourse B

I meet with friends and family

They shed their tears and hug me tight

For soon I will take my final flight

Their sight fades fast when I begin to board

I am feeling warmth like never before

I see an Angel in feathered flight

Neither a man nor a woman but oh so bright!

We speed through the heavens

Like two birds in flight

Booster rockets fire!

Propelling us into the light!

In a room filled with beings so familiar to me

I feel so happy and so very free

They lead me about to see the stars and the sun

And to visit with friends and family that I have known

When I look to a vision that is so loving and bright

With his hands on my shoulder, he fills me with light

Welcome home he said, you have done your best

Rest my child, and may I bless

Table of Contents

Michael Hobert Edwards

Introduction:

Now that you opened this book for the first time, why may I ask did you buy this book? Was it the title that captured your interest? Are you a paranormal researcher, investigator, or weekend enthusiast interested in adding Radio Sweep (Ghost Box) Electronic Voice Phenomena (EVP) to your list of tools? Do you want to know what happens when we die, where we go when we die, and what is it like there? Or perhaps do you just want to test this concept and process to see if it is really true that anyone can communicate with the dead using a hacked store bought or homemade radio along with a digital recorder?

Speaking to the Dead with Radios I will tell you is not this just another fish story to reel in readers for momentary mind entertainment. Communicating with the dead using a radio with recorder is achievable and any person can do it. You do not need to be a psychic, a medium or have any paranormal gifts to make contact with the dead using these devices, and that my friend is the luxury of this in that you do not have to pay someone else hundreds or even thousands of dollars to contact your deceased family members or friends as you can do it yourself in the privacy of your own home.

What is even more amazing is the dead, spirits, ghosts, whatever you want to call them are everywhere around us, and if you turn a recorder on anywhere, you will get messages from the dead. I found this out real quick when I first started to record. I always thought a house or a location had to be haunted in order for spirits to be present, and that I found is not true. The dead are everywhere! I remember talking to one of my sisters after I shared with her some recordings with my late father Hobert Collin Edwards, and she quickly said "Can daddy see me when I'm in the bathroom?", and I replied yes, he can see you anywhere you are, and he can hear you talking. That totally blew her mind!

So what does that really mean? They can see and hear us, but from where? My first thought was Dad was somehow meeting with me through let's say a portal type window, one in which he could see through and see and hear me, but I could not see nor hear him. But that belief changed one day after I recorded a message from dad that said "I was sittin inside Patrick's car when police pulled him for speeding, and they let him go". This recording happened right around the time that my son was in his first year in college, and when my wife asked my son about it he replied he was pulled over, and given a warning. This told me that my dad is here in spirit when he wants to be, and that he can see and hear everything.

Now how fair is that? They can see and hear us, but we can't see and hear them unless we have medium or psychic abilities. Learning the dead can see and hear us, and more especially after learning that I could hear them using Radio Sweep (Ghost Box) Electronic Voice Phenomena devices along with a digital or a tape recorder, my mind began to reel!

I realized this device was not just a toy to play with recording voices at home or at weekend paranormal investigations, but it could also be used to help change the world. It could be used by medical professionals to find answers needed for a cure. It could be used by space, aeronautical, ship, automotive, and factory engineers to ask the deceased that have access to or know how to develop non-polluting fuels to operate them. It could be used by law enforcement to communicate with crime victims to try and get the information needed to solve crimes. Radio Sweep (Ghost Box) EVP devices are tools!

Within this book I will teach you what Radio Sweep (Ghost Box) Electronic Voice Phenomena is all about which is using a simple digital scan radio I purchased from an electronics store, a radio that has been hacked or altered by cutting the mute wire or pin to enable the radio to scan or sweep stations un-muted continuously. The radio is used in conjunction with an external speaker to project the noise, and a digital recorder to record any paranormal messages in the form of electronic voice phenomena "EVP" that may sound within the noise of the radio as it scans or sweeps the stations un-muted. This process is known by many in the paranormal community as Radio Sweep (Ghost Box) Electronic Voice Phenomena (EVP).

In chapter one, I will outline and discuss in depth the history of Radio Sweep (Ghost Box) Electronic Voice Phenomena introducing you to some very exceptional radio sweep pioneers who have and continue to share their skills and methods in building radio sweep EVP devices from the ground up using radio electronic parts or hacking, taking apart existing store bought radios and altering their design to enable the radio to scan or sweep stations un-muted, and or use these devices as tools to help people.

In chapter two, I will teach you the concept of speaking to the dead with radios in which you can encounter the dead through real time spirit communication having a two way conversation hearing responses to your questions during the actual recording session, and not just later on playback using the traditional recorder only process most paranormal investigators use.

Chapter three is where you will learn which store bought radios can be hacked, made to work as a Radio

Sweep (Ghost Box) EVP device, and learn about key individuals you can contact directly to find out what radios are being hacked today and where to buy one.

In chapter four, I will teach you about unhappy spirits you may encounter while recording Radio Sweep (Ghost Box) EVP, how to recognize them, and how to deal with them. You will learn also about Technicians, kind and loving spirits whose sole purpose is to help ensure your recording sessions runs smoothly without issues.

Chapter five teaches you about preferred radio sweep equipment, manual sweep radios verses digital scan or sweep radios, and tape recorders verses digital recorders. Here I will also teach you how to make an appointment to record with the dead.

In chapter six, I will outline what encompasses a Radio Sweep (Ghost Box) EVP recording session. You will learn about the different recording session types you may engage in from the Show and They Tell session in which the dead tell you what you are asking them to identify, the Deceased Loved One recording session one in which you record with a deceased family, friend, or clients loved one to record messages they want their living family to know, the Known Deceased Missing Person in which you record with a deceased missing person to record information that may help solve their case, and you also will learn about the Paranormal Investigation recording session which involves recording messages with the dead at client location to learn more about the dead who reside there or learn more about the activity occurring affecting the property owner.

Chapter seven is where I will show you how to upload your digital recorder's wma file to your computer, and there on convert it to a wave file using NCH® software.

In chapter eight, I will teach you how to segment or break up your question with answer files, and teach you how to de-noise them if necessary.

Chapter nine which is one of the most important chapters in this book is where I will teach you how to classify recorded messages as Radio Traffic, Suspect Paranormal, and Paranormal. Like chapter eight, this is one of several critical steps in the process to get your files ready for transcription.

In chapter ten you will learn how to listen to and transcribe any recorded Suspect Paranormal or Paranormal messages into a Microsoft® Excel worksheet.

Preparing your files for yourself or a client in chapter eleven is where I will teach you how to assemble your recorded messages in a format the client or even you can easily read and listen to.

Chapter twelve is where I will share and discuss a variety of Deceased Loved One, Known Deceased Missing Person, and Paranormal Investigation cases I have recorded to give you an idea how you should expect cases of this type may proceed if you decide to engage a recording session of this type.

Lastly in chapter thirteen, which is another important chapter in this book, I will share with each of you some ideas I have what Radio Sweep (Ghost Box) EVP devices can be used for going forward.

Radio Sweep (Ghost Box) Electronic Voice Phenomena (EVP)

Radio Sweep (Ghost Box) EVP are believed to be messages from the dead that show up in the noise or raw audio of the radio scanning or sweeping stations, and these words which can be male, female, young or old sounding, animated or even electronic sounding are somehow assembled by the dead from the radio traffic into intelligible messages often in one or more words, short phrases or longer sentences. The often they occur and can be heard real time where they are loud enough that the person engaging the recording session can hear the message and respond back with an answer real time.

For me, I was at first a nonbeliever in this concept that is until I tested it myself. One day late 2007 while browsing the paranormal section at Barnes and Noble®, I stumbled upon a book written by a respected occult writer, Konstantinos. The title of the book, "Speak with the Dead" intrigued me so that I bought it with one purpose in mind which was to try and learn how to make contact with my late father, Hobert Collin Edwards.

Using the guidance from "Speak with the Dead", I tested the concept with my old worldwide Panasonic® AM/FM/SW manual sweep radio, and an old Sony® micro cassette tape recorder achieving some Radio Sweep (Ghost Box) EVP, but not with my father. Frustrated with having to continuously turn the manual radio dial to get results, I gave up, but later learned that there were other radios, digital scan radios that can sweep stations continuously by the click of a button, radios that could be altered by design and used to make contact with the dead.

In February 2008, while watching an airing of Paranormal State (PRS) ®, CASE FILE: 2007.11.43F - "The Asylum", my life changed forever! PRS® had invited Christopher Moon, a paranormal researcher who had been testing the controversial "Frank's Box", a ghost box known by many within the paranormal community as the "telephone to the dead".

A "Frank's Box" a name coined by Christopher Moon himself, is a Radio Sweep (Ghost Box) EVP device built by a gifted man named Frank Sumption. Frank has built over 100 Radio Sweep (Ghost Box) EVP devices, selling several to friends and peers within the paranormal community to use and test.

A Frank's Box is designed to scan or sweep AM and FM stations continuously un-muted. According to Frank Sumption as well as others, spirit entities need something that contains elements of human speech which is believed to be raw audio, and a source of raw audio is being broadcast everyday by radio stations around the world. A "Frank's Box" sweeps across these radio broadcasts producing an endless stream of bits of human speech, music, and white noise with white noise being less important. It is believed that the spirit entities somehow use this raw audio to communicate with us in the form of voices. For example, when you play the game of scrabble, you use letters from the board game to form words, and with Radio Sweep (Ghost Box) EVP it is believed the dead somehow use raw audio to assemble words often in the form of one or more words, short phrases or longer sentences to communicate with the living.

When using these Radio Sweep (Ghost Box) EVP devices, real time spirit communication (RTSC) with the dead can and does happen, meaning you can ask a question and get an answer to that question real time during some sessions.

Frank Sumption crafted his first Radio Sweep (Ghost Box) EVP device in 2002 from spare radio and computer parts.

After watching the show, thoughts raced through my mind of getting one of Frank Sumption's radios, so I could try and contact my father. Through the show's website, I contacted Frank Sumption to inquire how I could get a radio like his. Frank informed me that I could either build a Ghost Box radio from the bottom up like he did, and he would gladly give me a copy of his design plans, or that I could simply buy a $25.00 radio and alter its design to scan stations un-muted.

Having no electronics background, I opted for what has become known as the Shack Hack 12-469 digital scan radio which can be seen at http://www.keyportparanormal.com/hackableradiosghostbox.html, or you can Google® the words Shack Hack 12-469.

In addition to the radio, I also purchased an Olympus® digital recorder, and an external speaker to hook up to the radio which by design has an internal speaker enabling the radio to be used with headphones or ear buds only. The external speaker is necessary to project the raw audio noise when scanning stations un-muted.

After I was set up with my equipment, Frank Sumption invited me to join his EVP Yahoo® web discussion group at http://tech.groups.yahoo.com/group/EVP-ITC/, so I could engage dialog with other members to learn how to use the Radio Sweep (Ghost Box) EVP device. It was through this Yahoo® group, where I met some very wonderful and very talented people like Steve Hultay of "Keyport Paranormal®", Bruce Halliday of "Inside the Box RTSC Ghost Box Research" each who along with Frank Sumption taught me how to use the Radio Sweep (Ghost Box) EVP device.

Chapter One:
The History of Radio Sweep
(Ghost Box) Electronic Voice Phenomena

Before I discuss and share my recording and transcription process as well as share and discuss some of my client case experiences recording Radio Sweep (Ghost Box) EVP, I would first like to familiarize each of you with a brief history.

Electronic Voice Phenomena, (EVP), also known as Extremely Low Voice Phenomena are recorded voices that show up on magnetic tape or digital recorders. As for where the concept of EVP began or better yet who invented it, this is a topic still being discussed.

2000 After testing a young German software engineer's EVP making program, Frank Sumption an American paranormal researcher from Colorado got the idea to create his own EVP device using Radio Sweep technology. By his own design, Frank using spare radio parts from electronics stores built a device that produces random voltage to create raw audio from an AM radio tuner. Raw audio as explained by Frank is comprised of bits of human speech, music and noise, and a good source of raw audio is a radio with its tuning sweeping across the entire bands of AM, FM, or even Short-wave. The sweep can be random, linear, or manual sweep. Within the paranormal community Frank's device goes by two names which are "Frank's Box" or a "Ghost Box". The "Frank's Box", a name coined by Christopher Moon, sweeps across these radio broadcasts producing an endless stream of bits of human speech, music and white noise with the white noise being less important. It is believed that the spirit entities somehow use this raw audio to communicate with us in the form of voices.

Frank has built several different versions of his radio sweep Ghost Box selling the devices to his peers to test during investigations or personal research. His contributions to this field of study have reached a global level sharing his design plans, personal experiences and guidance with others. As noted in the introduction of this book, Frank Sumption has built over 100 "Frank's Boxes". To learn more about "Frank's Box" you can join Frank Sumption's EVP/ITC Yahoo® web group http://tech.groups.yahoo.com/group/EVP-ITC/?yguid=338683728 . To see photographs of a myriad of Franks Boxes, friend me on face book® at http://www.facebook.com/SDWRSpeakingToTheDeadWithRadios?sk=photos and view my photo album

2002 Juli Velazquez, a Chicago area native is Editor –in-Chief of The Haunted Herald Newspaper; President & Founder of I.S.P.I. (International Society of Paranormal

Investigators). Previously she worked as CEO of Paranormal Underworld, and also worked as an independent writer being featured in such publications as Haunted Times Magazine, Haunted Indiana and Ghost Magazine.

Juli has been known as one of the leading researchers in two way real time spirit communication, and holds the honor of being the second women in the world to own a Frank's Box. She was elected one out of nineteen paranormal investigators across the country to beta testing some of the latest technology in paranormal equipment, the Paranormal Puck and Ovilus . Her first introduction to Radio Sweep (Ghost Box) Electronic Voice Phenomena came about when she visited the haunted Mason House in Bensport, Iowa with another paranormal investigator, Christopher Moon. Juli has since used Radio Sweep (Ghost Box) EVP devices as an aid in helping solve missing person cases.

Having experienced unique opportunities investigating famous haunted locations such as the Sallie House, Mansfield Reformatory and Waverly Hills Sanitarium, touching on the darker side of the paranormal, Juli has been witness to demonic entities, and has also suffered physical attacks during her quests. In December 2010, Juli was featured in the movie "The Possessed" on SyFy and Children of the Grave II.

Juli currently travel across the country to locations alleged to be haunted, where data and evidence is collected in her quest for proving the afterlife. She has had two near death experiences, knowing first hand that there is more to death, than what we can see. As a result of crossing over, she was blessed with the gifts of clairvoyance, clairaudient and clairsentient (Empathic) being one of her strongest senses.

2004 Christopher Moon had his first paranormal experience at the age of seven. Daily occurrences from that time on included objects disappearing and reappearing; doors opening and closing on their own fruition, strange shadows and light anomalies, and nightly haunted sonnets on the family's one hundred year old grand piano. He also discovered that he had a definite psychic/medium sense, and began doing remedial paranormal investigations at a mere 12 years of age.

A musician by trade, Moon spent many years playing in and touring with Rock and Metal bands. Eventually his interest in the paranormal overtook his passion for music, and Moon chose to become a full-time professional investigator.

Wanting the paranormal community and general public to become aware of what he had known for years, that the paranormal existed and could be documented, Christopher partnered with his father, a devout skeptic, in developing a magazine that would represent a truly balanced view of the subject. Consequently, Haunted Times Magazine was born in 2004.

Prior to publishing the first issue of Haunted Times Magazine, Christopher, seeing a true need for formal paranormal education, opened the first public educational event entitled Ghost Hunter University. These one of a kind events are held at various haunted locations around the United States. It includes fully interactive seminars titled "Ghost Hunting 101" and "Ghost Hunting 102".

While searching for magazine staff in 2004, Christopher was contacted by an engineer by trade, Frank Sumption, who claimed to have a device that allowed two-way audio communication with the dead. Skeptical, Christopher met with Mr. Sumption at his workshop for a demonstration. Christopher was astounded to find that the device that Frank Sumption had built was actually designed through the E.V.P. (Electronic Voice Phenomena) of deceased scientists. It quickly became obvious to Christopher what Frank Sumption had done; he had completed the infamous Thomas Edison Telephone to the Dead. Frank graciously offered to give Christopher one of the machines to use in the field. He accepted, and first used the device while investigating the famous Sallie House in Atchison, Kansas. The machine worked flawlessly, and Christopher and his team collected real time E.V.P. evidence directly from the spirits in the house. The Telephone to the Dead, which Christopher refers to this device as, formally referred to as "Frank's Box", has become an invaluable tool in Christopher's paranormal research.

In March 2007, Christopher was invited to lecture about his research at the Ghost Chasers Weekend Conference in Savannah, Georgia. It was at this conference, where Christopher realized his talents using the Telephone to the Dead, would be needed in more than a paranormal research capacity. His presentation quickly turned into a public demonstration of the Telephone to the Dead. One by one, attendees asked to speak with loved ones who had passed. Surprisingly, even to Christopher, these requests were met with comforting, and sometimes vital messages.

Since that conference, Christopher has been asked repeatedly to use the Telephone to the Dead to perform personal, private readings for people worldwide. Although reluctant at first, Christopher realized the impact he had on the attendees at the Savannah conference, and decided to begin using his psychic and medium abilities, as well as the Telephone to the Dead, to perform private readings to the public.

Christopher tours college campuses around the country, lecturing on his ghost hunting techniques and providing positive evidence, as well as interactive investigations using the Telephone to the Dead to many excited students, eager to learn more about the paranormal. His television appearances and interviews include, most notably, Tru-Tv Network's "Door to the Dead", NBC's "Today Show", A & E Network's "Paranormal State", and the Travel Channel's "Most Extreme Places to Stay", as well as numerous ABC, CBS, NBC, CW (formally the WB), and FOX affiliate stations around the country. He has appeared on many nationwide radio programs, such as Coast to Coast AM with George Noory, Coast to Coast AM with Ian Punnit, Kiss FM's nationally syndicated morning show with Johnjay and Rich, Providence's WPRO FM morning show with Giovanni and Kim, Long Island's WRCN morning show with Dave and Glenn, TAPS Radio Beyond Reality, KHOW Radio, Denver, with Peter Boyles, Canada's Richard Syrett Show, BBS Radio – Beyond Two Worlds Radio Show, Clear Channel Radio's Real Paranormal Talk, A.P.S.R. Paranormal Talk Radio, Ghostology Radio Show, Shadows in the Dark Radio Show, X-Zone, BUFO, Spooky South coast Radio Program, Late Night Live Radio Program, and many more. Contact Chris through his web site at http://www.chrismoonpsychic.com/Chris_Moon_Psychic/Home.html.

2005 Bruce Halliday, an American EVP pioneer from New Jersey with over fifteen years experience in the paranormal started testing manual sweep radios in 2005. In 2007 his friend Steve Hultay introduced him to a "Joe's Box" a radio sweep EVP device built for Steve by a man named Joe Cioppi. Joe built this box based on similar design of Frank

Sumption's ghost boxes. Bruce purchased the "Joe's Box" from Joe Cioppi to begin working with this Ghost Box to receive Live Spirit Communication.

At this time Bruce already had a Frank's Box 12 given to him by Frank Sumption to test, and he later received another Frank's Box #29. Bruce Halliday has tested and hacked a variety of different radios all inclusive of Frank's Boxes, Joe's Boxes, and all the shack hacks.

From 2008 through 2009 while working as moderator for Steve Hultay's RTSC Yahoo® web group. Bruce contributed his time and money serving as a respected leader in Radio Sweep (Ghost Box) EVP device design, testing and education teaching both current and new paranormal enthusiast how to hack and use the radios to capture EVP.

On April 6, 2009, Bruce Halliday founded his own EVP Yahoo® group Inside the Box RTSC Ghost Box Research which is located at this web page. http://tech.groups.yahoo.com/group/inside_the_box_rtsc_g host_box_research/?yguid=338683728 In 2010 Bruce Halliday hacked a manufactured radio, a Jensen® SAB-55, and he developed an exceptional Radio Sweep (Ghost Box) EVP process that both beginners and avid enthusiast could use to communicate with the dead. This particular radio by design is an arm band radio in which the user can strap it to their arm with Velcro straps, and walk or jog while listening to the radio.

The Halliday Hack as it has been coined has proven to be an exceptional contender up against the Shack Hack 12-469 radio, a popular hard to find radio no longer in production. The Halliday Hack has done so well in Ghost Box communication, that it has even experienced air time on the new television show ©1999-2011 The Haunted . On

October 24, 2010 the Halliday Hack was used to receive communication from a spirit of a young boy who was believed to have been shot to death in his home. A psychic medium was brought by "The Paranormal Environmental Explanations from Research group" (P.E.E.R) to perform a psychic reading in the home, and this psychic experienced a vision of the boy being shot in the basement of his home. Using the Halliday Hack along with a digital recorder, a paranormal message was recorded from a spirit that said "I am shot!" which validates what the psychic experienced in their reading.

Bruce Halliday continues to test and hack new radios, as well as to teach newcomers interested in learning how to record Ghost Box communication using Radio Sweep (Ghost Box) EVP devices. ". You can reach Bruce Halliday through his web page http://www.insidetheboxrtscghostbox.com/jensensab55hack.html

2007 In 2007, an American EVP pioneer under a fictitious name posted instructions how to create a Radio Sweep (Ghost Box) EVP device from a Radio Shack® radio by clipping the mute pin allowing the radio to scan stations un-muted, and through this simple discovery, the "Shack Hack" was born.

Paranormal enthusiast who once depended on paranormal television shows to feed their insatiable appetite, could now with a small investment communicate with the dead either in the privacy of their home, in the field for an investigation, at haunted locations, or at cemeteries with friends, family, or even at local meet-up groups. Why pay a medium to contact your dead father when you can do that yourself in the privacy of your home with a Shack Hack?

With the Shack Hack discovery now in full view, other great EVP pioneers soon followed taking up where others left off working to perfect or simplify the process. The Shack Hack discovery clearly became the catalyst that prompted the creation of Yahoo® web groups where like individuals could upload their EVP files for others to listen, and the hack discovery also prompted the need for education from how one hacks the radio to make it scan stations un-muted, to what type of radios could actually be hacked, and how to engage a recording session.

2007 Mike Coletta, an American paranormal enthusiast and founder of UFO Geek.com became one of those admired individuals responsible for creating You-Tube® educational videos has tremendously helped to propel Shack Hack knowledge and usage to a much larger audience than those that had the electronic skills to build, for example, a Frank's Box from scratch.

Mike provides You-Tube® video education to anyone that wants to know how to take radios that can be hacked apart, how to cut the mute pin or wire that will allow the radio to scan stations un-muted, and then how to put the radio back together again. To contact Mike Coletta, go to his web site here http://www.ufogeek.com/.

2007 Steve Hultay a young EVP pioneer from Keyport, NJ – USA and founder of Keyport Paranormal®, at very young age took up interest in the paranormal when he started seeing and feeling things he couldn't explain.

His interest led him from experimenting with Ouija boards, dowsing with rods and pendulums to two-way box communication using a device he was introduced to called an "EVP Listener". What this device was attempting to do was pick up the same magnetic frequencies as an EMF meter and convert them into audible sounds. The EVP Listener tried to capture a different frequency to listen to other than our own. This didn't seem to be what Steve was looking for and his search started once again for yet another communication tool for EVP or Electronic Voice Phenomena. Steve wanted to try and communicate and help earthbound spirits who may be listening to our side and possibly answer some questions.

His sister Tracy Hultay sent Steve an e-mail with a link to a piece of equipment called "Frank's Box". This is the most popular of all of the boxes in the Radio Sweep paranormal community today. The schematics were offered to the public by Frank Sumption himself, and they are available on line for anyone to attempt and build one themselves.

Learning there were only a limited supply of these devices with most being given to paranormal researcher Christopher Moon of Haunted Times Magazine, Steve Hultay decided to attend one of his Christopher Moon's Ghost Hunter Universities to see "Frank's Box" in action, and through this experience he linked into one of Frank Sumption's web sites to learn more about the ghost box and to read over the design schematics of the device listening to available electronic voice phenomena recorded using the box.

Within Frank Sumption's web site Steve Hultay read a comment posted by a retired engineer named Joe Cioppi. Steve e-mailed Mr. Cioppi and to ask him if he would build a "Frank's box" for him based on the web site's ghost box schematics, and Joe responded that he was already working on his own breadboard with an FM chip that would work similar to Frank's design. Joe offered Steve an opportunity to try it out at cost for parts and a fair price for labor. Hultay accepted Joe's offer, and started testing Prototype #1 which in Steve's mind turned out to be a flop. Steve felt the sweep rate was way too slow and picked up several FM radio voices in full before sweeping to the next. Steve returned the device and explained to Joe what he felt he should be hearing, and Joe updated Box #1 with a new design to sweep at a much faster rate.

While Steve Hultay was busy testing the re-designed Box #1, Joe Cioppi had begun work on Box #2 which by design had a much faster sweep rate. When Steve met with Joe to pick up and test Box #2, they both sat down in his kitchen for hours and collaborated on different ideas. While Joe's Box #2 proved to be a success allowing Steve to hear answers to questions that he could not explain, he started to record even more with the dead and found through listening there were a lot more paranormal messages from the dead than what he was able to hear real time. Through these experiences and continued research Steve decided to start his own internet web page which he named Keyport Paranormal®.

In June of 2007, Steve Hultay also joined Frank Sumption's EVP-ITC – EVP and ITC discussion group forum on Yahoo® mainly as a springboard to upload and share his radio sweep ghost box EVP messages from the dead with others and to also offer newcomers to this field of study other radio alternatives, manufactured radios that could be hacked and used in recording messages from the dead. Sumption, listened to some of Steve Hultay's audio files and stated he felt Steve's files were excellent and possibly even better than messages recorded using a "Frank's box".

Sumption was so impressed by Steve, he offered Steve a "Frank's Box" to test which was FB #13, but after thoroughly testing Frank's Box #13, Steve concluded that the ghost box was not what he expected as it was very noisy picking up a lot of interference perhaps because it was not battery operated. Not wanting to bother Frank Sumption about the unexpected noise, Steve shipped Franks Box #13 to Joe Cioppi to alter its design making it battery operated. This design change, sadly did not work as expected, so Steve shipped it back to Frank Sumption who built Steve a replacement "Frank's Box" which he named Box #27.

After about 6 months of hard research working with both "Frank's Box" and other hacked radio sweep ghost box EVP devices, feeling alone in his quest, Steve contacted a local paranormal investigator and friend named Bruce Halliday, and told Bruce about the concept of radio sweep ghost box communication. Not initially sold on the idea, Bruce agreed to give it a try, and began work with Steve testing a Frank's box #12 and "Joe's Box" #3.

On March 8, 2008 Steve Hultay founded RTSC-Real Time Spirit Communication http://tech.groups.yahoo.com/group/RTSC/, a Yahoo® web group dedicated to capturing EVP from non-traditional methods. Steve asked Bruce Halliday to moderate the group, and the two worked to assist in teaching others how to set up EVP devices and how to record for paranormal messages.

Both men worked together as a team until April 6, 2009 when Bruce Halliday formed his own Yahoo® web group called Inside the Box RTSC Ghost Box Research.

Steve Hultay's contributions to the research and study of Electronic Voice Phenomena have been one of continued research hacking and testing different radios, as well as providing a place where both newcomers and seasoned veterans of Radio Sweep EVP can post files for discussion and guidance.

In 2008 Steve Hultay initiated start-up of a weekly radio show called RTSC – Talk Radio to further help get the word out about Radio Sweep EVP.

Steve Hultay continues to hack and build EVP devices and has discussed Radio Sweep EVP through lectures as well as engaged in a TV appearance recording an episode of the Discovery Channel® "Mystery Hunters" where he recorded Radio Sweep EVP with the late Thomas Edison. To contact Steve Hultay, go to his Yahoo® web group located here http://tech.groups.yahoo.com/group/RTSC/.

2007 Joseph A. Cioppi Sr. a retired engineer from Doylestown, PA was so intrigued by Chris Moon's demonstration of Frank Sumption's "Frank's Box" on Coast to Coast AM® and on You Tube®, that he acquired a copy of Frank Sumption's Radio Sweep (Ghost Box) design schematics and attempted to build one from the ground up, but stopped when he discovered a Phillips® Electronics FM tuner chip that proved much easier to implement.

This chip had built in features that were more suitable for random selection of radio stations. Just after he successfully bread-boarded a working FM random sweep circuit, he received a call from Steve Hultay, founder of Keyport Paranormal®, who asked Joe to build him a

Frank's Box. Joe agreed to do the job, but noted to Steve that had developed a much better design and could package it for Steve while he worked on the Frank's Box build. Hultay mentioned to Joe that he did not believe a slow sweep would be accepted by the skeptics, so Joe changed the timing components to give a wider adjustment range with a faster rate to a slower rate. Hultay also wanted a louder audio output, so his friends could hear the random messages clearly.

Early on Joe Cioppi numbered his Radio Sweep (Ghost Box) units which were called "Joe's Box", but he has built so many now that he stopped numbering them. Many of "Joe's Boxes" are now being used within the United States, Scotland, Australia, Mexico, and Canada. All components of this homemade box are built into surplus CB radio shells. To contact or to learn more about Joe Cioppi go to his web site at http://www.freewebs.com/joecioppi/ which is called Philadelphia Spirit Communication.

2007 Michael Edwards of Cary, North Carolina, began his EVP avocation using the process known as Radio Sweep (Ghost Box) Electronic Voice Phenomena to record messages from the dead. One day while browsing the paranormal section at Barnes and Noble®, Michael stumbled upon a book written by a respected occult writer, Konstantinos who authored a book titled "Speak with the Dead". This book intrigued Michael so much that he bought it with one purpose in mind which was to try and learn how to make contact with his late father, Hobert Collin Edwards.

Using the guidance from "Speak with the Dead", Michael tested the concept and process using his old worldwide Panasonic® AM/FM/SW manual sweep radio, and an old Sony® micro cassette tape recorder achieving some Radio Sweep (Ghost Box) EVP, but not with his father.

Frustrated with having to continuously turn the manual radio dial to get results, Michael gave up. At this time, however, he was not aware that other radios, digital scan radios that scan or sweep stations continuously by the click of a button could also be used to make contact with the dead.

In February 2008, while watching an airing of Paranormal State (PRS), A&E Television®, and CASE FILE: 2007.11.43F - "The Asylum", Michael's life changed forever! PRS had invited Christopher Moon, a paranormal researcher who had been testing the controversial "Frank's Box", known by many within the paranormal community as the "telephone to the dead".

A "Frank's Box" is a Radio Sweep (Ghost Box) EVP device built by a gifted man named Frank Sumption. Frank has built over 100 of these devices, giving away or selling some to friends and peers within the paranormal community to use and test.

After watching the show, thoughts raced through Michael's mind of getting one of Frank Sumption's radios, so he could try and contact his father. Through the show's web-site, he contacted Frank Sumption to inquire how he could get a radio like Frank's.

Frank Sumption informed Michael that he could either build a radio like his from the ground up like he did, and he would gladly give Michael a copy of his design plans, or that Michael could simply buy a $25.00 electronics store radio and alter it to scan stations un-muted.

Having no electronics background, Michael opted to buy and hack a Radio Shack® model 12-469 digital scan radio which can be seen at http://www.keyportparanormal.com/hackableradiosghostbox.html, or you can Google® the words shack hack 12-469. Since this model radio has an internal speaker, so you need to buy an external speaker to project the noise. After Michael purchased an Olympus® model WS-100 digital recorder, he joined Frank Sumption's EVP-ITC Yahoo® group to learn how to record and listen to any paranormal messages.

In February of 2008 when Michael Edwards first turned on his hacked Shack Hack 12-469 radio, he heard and recorded a real time message that said "Mike Edwards!", and when Michael asked who that was that said his name, he received a real time response of "Christian".

Michael continued testing the radio holding up items and asking any dead in his room to name the item, and during one of his recordings when he held up a carved wooden dolphin and asked the dead to name it, he received a real time message of "Fish, Fish, Dolphin, and Dolphin".

After learning how to better record and listen to Radio Sweep (Ghost Box) EVP, Michael began to record paranormal messages with deceased missing children to try and help assist missing person advocates working with police. Using his radio and a digital recorder, Michael teamed with a Chicago area Medium, Juli Velazquez, to help record for any information concerning a missing teen.

For this particular case, Juli using her remote viewing skill pinpointed a location near where the teen was last seen, and Michael began recording for any EVP messages from the believed to be deceased teen. While recording with the teen, Michael recorded messages of the word "Receipts" that were repeated several times in different recordings. When a private search team went into the area associated with the recording session, a bag of receipts was found by the search focal, and these receipts belonged to the victim. A subsequent search of the area also revealed other evidence.

In July 2008 Michael founded a Yahoo® group EVP-ITC-SDWR-Speaking to the Dead with Radios at http://tech.groups.yahoo.com/group/EVP-ITC-SDWR-SpeakingToTheDeadWithRadios-/?yguid=338683728 . The group was initially formed as an active group allowing members to post and discuss Radio Sweep (Ghost Box) EVP messages, but it is now set up as a place for both current and future clients to listen to messages from the dead Michael has recorded.

In February 2009 Michael teemed with a group of Radio Sweep (Ghost Box) EVP as well as the traditional Recorder only EVP enthusiast to try and use these EVP devices to contact a deceased and renowned cancer researcher to try and get him to provide answers to three questions posed by a North Carolina Cancer researcher.

Of all the recorded messages we received, only one recorded message captured by a team member using a digital recorder could actually be tied to a medical term. The question posed, "What are the Kinase/phosphates responsible for the addition/removal of the cytoplasmic retention phosphorylation on MPF (The CDK1/Cyclin B Complex)?", and the answer recorded from the deceased cancer researcher phonetically sounded like it said "Check the Zygotes".

Through this experience Michael realized since the

team did not have medical backgrounds especially in this field of study, they may have missed other terms that because of their lack of knowledge in medical terms, they would not have understood them phonetically as they sounded.

In April 2011, Michael formed a face book® group named "The Worldwide Radio Sweep – Ghost Box EVP Alliance. This group present day January 2nd, 2012 is currently at two hundred thirty members and is a mix of people from around the world who record for messages from the dead using either hacked store bought radios, or they build their own radios from the ground up. Members post Radio Sweep (Ghost Box) EVP recordings from the dead, they engage in discussion about radio sweep, share paranormal photographs, and share and discuss their experiences and encounters while performing paranormal investigations.

Michael formed this group to bring together veteran Radio Sweep (Ghost Box) EVP enthusiast from around the world to share their methods and processes, and to also provide a place in which any new comers, people out there that have an interest in learning about radio sweep, to review and listen to veteran postings, and to be able to exchange dialog with veteran ghost box radio sweepers learning how they too can learn to communicate with their loved ones.

Present day 2012, Michael continues to record Radio Sweep (Ghost Box) EVP connecting families with their loved ones as well as teaching others how to record using these devices in the privacy of their homes. To contact Michael Hobert Edwards, reach him through his Yahoo® web group located at URL http://tech.groups.yahoo.com/group/EVP-ITC-SDWR-SpeakingToTheDeadWithRadios-/?yguid=338683728 or through face book® at The Worldwide Radio Sweep - Ghost Box EVP Alliance at this URL http://www.facebook.com/groups/102193593178906/

2009 Gary Galka of Connecticut who lost his daughter in a car accident designed and constructed a Spirit Box, a device that uses radio sweep technology to communicate with the dead. Upon testing the device, Gary recorded a paranormal message from his daughter that said "hi daddy, I love you." The Radio Sweep device Model P-SB7 is the first production Spirit Box device offered to the paranormal community. It is a mini size Spirit Box the size of an MP3 player. The P-SB7 made its premier debut on Ghost Adventures "LIVE" show. The show was broadcast from the Trans-Allegheny Lunatic Asylum on October 30, 2009 where the P-SB7 was used by Chris Fleming, a Sensitive, Paranormal Investigator and expert in the Paranormal field. The P-SB7 provided responses to his questions in real time over a 40 minute segment of the show. When used by a properly trained individual, under certain circumstances, the P-SB7 will provide results similar that of an EVP recorder, but in real time. Since then, it has become very popular and can be seen frequently on Ghost Adventures and Psychic Kids where Zak and Chris Fleming continue to receive consistent relevant responses to specific questions. The P-SB7 utilizes a millisecond adjustable forward or reverse frequency "sweep" technique coupled with a proprietary high frequency synthetic noise or "white noise" distributed between frequency steps. The New 2011 model now offers an enhanced FM frequency sweep which includes an additional 119 new frequencies from 76MHz to 87.9MHz. No other hack box or modified radio currently offers this. A seven step adjustable sweep rate provides user flexibility based on individual technique and session circumstances. There are two discreet audio outputs; (1)

15mW Earphone, and (1) 250mW Speaker. A bright EL back light display with manual ON/OFF select is ideal for viewing in the dark. The P-SB7 uses three "AAA" batteries. The P-SB7 is intended to be used by professional investigators to help promote the field of Paranormal ITC Research.

Chapter Two:
Speaking to the Dead with Radios

Speaking to the dead with radios obviously is the name of my book, but what actually does that mean in layman terms. Do I have a radio that I turn on to have a two way conversation with the dead, for example, like using a CB Radio? Well no, not exactly. The radio is just a just a tool used in the process to help record paranormal messages or Electronic Voice Phenomena (EVP).

As you learned from reading the history of Radio Sweep (Ghost Box) EVP, there are different ways and devices to record and capture EVP. Radio Sweep (Ghost Box) EVP as noted during my introduction, culminates using a manufactured or homemade radio that has been altered to scan or sweep stations un-muted which creates a medium the dead somehow use to formulate messages within that noise of the radio scanning stations, and those paranormal messages somehow get picked up by a tape or digital recorder. I personally believe the dead capture words within the noise of the radio scanning stations to form messages in the form of one or more words, phrases or sentences as one would use the game of scrabble to form words. For this reason, I believe messages tend to sound male, female, childlike, elderly, raspy, an even electronic sounding.

Unlike what I call the traditional EVP message which culminates from using a tape or a digital recorder only where you ask questions and do not hear any messages until play back, quite often when using the Radio Sweep (Ghost Box) EVP method during certain types of recording sessions, one can hear the messages "Real Time" during the recording process.

Real Time Spirit Communication (RTSC)

One of the luxuries of having and using a Radio Sweep (Ghost Box) EVP device, is you can often hear paranormal responses to your questions of the dead real time. Real Time Spirit Communication or (RTSC) coined by Steve Hultay of Keyport Paranormal®, simply means once you turn that radio and recorder on, if you ask your question and hear an answer to your question while the recording session is in process that form of communication is coined real time. You are in a sense having a two way conversation with the dead.

For example, during one of my Radio Sweep (Ghost Box) EVP recordings at Ferry Plantation Home, Virginia Beach, VA, several of us asked the dead what holiday the spirits in the home liked best, and we heard a real time audio voice message heard by everyone in the room that said "Christmas". Hearing that response in just about every room in the house, we later asked why they liked Christmas so much, and the next real time response we heard real time was "Because of the Presents".

To further explain RTSC; let's say that you reading this book are a paranormal investigator who assists families as does the T.A.P.S® team of Warwick, RI. In your process you only use digital recorders, and do not use Radio Sweep (Ghost Box) EVP devices. Under your current process, when you walk the client's property and ask questions, you have to wait until later after the investigation is over to listen to the recorder to see if you have recorded any paranormal messages, or EVP. If you add a Radio Sweep (Ghost Box) EVP device with your recorder, if the conditions are right, you now have the ability to communicate real time in a two way conversation with the dead. If you get a real time response, you can then ask more questions right there on the spot whereas using your current process you would not know what the dead said until after you have left the client's home, and listened later for any messages on play back.

One of my first RTSC EVP recordings I received occurred when I turned the radio on for the first time, and this message said "Mike Edwards". A spirit actually called out my name, and when I asked who he was, I got a message that was not real time that said Christian. When I asked again "who are you that called me, I got another real time message that said "Hello Michael" from a British sounding male voice. Hearing my name called out like that real time is what got me hooked like a fish into this field of study.

After I received this first real time message, and knowing that some dead person was in my room that could see and hear me, one that I could not see, I started arranging Radio Sweep (Ghost Box) EVP recordings with any dead spirits that wanted to tell me the name of certain items. I found that by holding up items in my hand, simple house hold items, and asking any dead in my room to tell me the name of the item, I was able to hear more real time messages.

Real time messages can be the dead answering a question you asked, or they can be the dead saying something to you or asking you a question. The following are some examples of real time messages I have recorded over the years, messages that were so loud I heard them while the hacked radio was scanning stations.

- Mike Edwards!
- Hello Michael!
- I'm here at Mike Edwards house
- Michael we touched you
- There is a cat on your lap
- I miss you
- I love you
- All of us
- It's a girl
- I did not kill her
- Bang! He shot me!
- Christmas
- They hung them
- Opossum
- I went bowling
- I was fat and nobody told me
- Tell Ruth I love my family
- That dumb deer, I saw him standing there
- I did
- The little
- CRX
- Tums
- Tell her he loved to see the ocean
- He had you for a month. His duct tape
- We shall save your mother

- Dolphin
- Husband
- I loved my husband
- Kids were hunting for me

I know that is a lot of real time messages, but I have a ton more, and way too many to list here. Real time messages when they occur provide you the recorder the opportunity to respond back, and this type of communication is a must when you use these devices as a tool to try and get information.

Imagine your father has passed, and before he died he told you to not forget about his coin collection. He is in the hospital bed, and you are sitting beside him, and he is fading in an out, and this time is a very emotional time for the two of you as you and he know death is near.

After the funeral, and perhaps some time later, you and the family are preparing to sell his house. While going through all of his belongings packing away his stuff in boxes for Good Will®, it hits you! Where is the coin collection? Oh my God, you say to yourself, the house has been sold, and we have to be out of here by next Friday!

If you just use a recorder only and you try and establish communication with your dad, you will not know what he said until later when you play it back, and even if you play it back later and the answer is not there, you will have to make another appointment with dad, and ask him more questions, and continue this process over and over again until the coin collection is found.

Under the right conditions, and in truth what those conditions actually are no one really knows, if you use a Radio Sweep (Ghost Box) EVP device used in conjunction with your recorder, if you hear your father speaking to you real time, you can respond back at that moment in time. Sure you still may have to engage in more than one recording with him, but having that two way conversation with him to try and find the coin collection can make the experience a lot easier than if you just used a recorder and play back what he may have said at a later date and time.

Below I will lay out what a real time recording session with your dad might sound like to try and find the coin collection. In this example below, I am only going to list out the real time responses you may have heard, and later I will discuss the other messages that got recorded that were not real time.

Question: Hello is my father John Wayne here today?

Response: Yes!

Question: Dad we are trying to find your coin collection. Do you know where it is?

Response: It___shelf___I love you

Question: OK Dad, I heard shelf, and I love you too. What shelf?

Response: It is by_____wood box

During this recording with your dad to try and find the location of his coin collection, you heard real time the following words which are "it, shelf, I love you, it is by, wood box". This was a good recording session. Now you know the coin collection is on a shelf somewhere, but you and your wife already searched the entire house, and did not find it. Furthermore, the house and garage are now completely empty, and all that is left to do is have the cleaning people come in to clean the house before the real estate closing.

What you the reader just read is a typical real time spirit communication dialog with a deceased person or spirit, however, there is more information you missed hearing during that recording session. You have yet to hear the lower sounding messages that occurred before and after the real time messages, and these messages are very important, and if you listen to them, you may not have to do additional recordings with dad to try and find the coins.

Going back to this fictional recording session I just laid out for you as an example, let's now go back, but using head phones, and if need be use some audio editing program to perhaps block the lower sounding messages that occurred before and after the real time message, and raise the volume a bit. After doing the above, below is how the recording session with messages from your dad looks now. bold text indicates the lower sounding words you did not hear real time.

Question: Hello is my father John Wayne here today?

Response: Yes!

Question: Dad we are trying to find your coin collection. Do you know where it is?

Response: It **is on the** shelf **in the attic**. I love you

Question: OK Dad, I heard shelf, and I love you too. What shelf?

Response: It is by **the window in a** wood box

Now by going back and listening to everything your father really said to you, and not just listening to the real time messages, you have the right information now to find the coin collection.

Real time spirit communication means you can hear the dead speaking to you during the recording session enabling you the ability to respond back to them with additional questions, however, I want each of you reading this book to understand to truly understand everything your loved one or any spirit is saying to you, you must also listen to all the lower sounding messages that occur before and after the real time messages. If you do not take the time to listen to them, even to raise the volume a bit to better hear them, in net you have neglected to hear everything your loved one, the loved one of a client, the deceased missing crime victim or any dead at the paranormal investigation location, really said to you.

By neglecting to hear it all, and if the recording session is one in which you are trying to find information that is ultimately going to help the living or solve a crime, you are wasting the spirit's time by having them come to your home for repeat visits.

Think of it this way, imagine you are a police detective, and you bring in a witness to a crime, and the witness tells you information about the case, and they answer any questions you may have. Imagine you are not listening to them as intently as you should, and you are also not writing down everything that person said. If you keep making appointments with that witness to keep coming back to you for more sessions, you are wasting their time, and after too many appointments with you, they may stop coming.

What I just said to you, actually happened to me while recording Radio Sweep (Ghost Box) EVP recording sessions with a particular deceased crime victim. At that time, I had not developed the process I use today, and was just listening to the entire question with answer file without segmenting it into smaller files. I missed hearing a lot of lower sounding messages only focusing on the real time messages, and after a myriad of repeat appointments with this deceased crime victim, during one recording session the spirit made an angry statement that he already told me what I wanted to know, and he never came to my house again.

In this book, I will teach you a specialized process I personally use to discern, listen to, and transcribe Radio Sweep (Ghost Box) Electronic Voice Phenomena messages, more especially messages that occur before and after a real time message. I will also share with each of you some of my personal experiences and some actual cases I recorded using this device.

To listen to some of my exceptional Radio Sweep (Ghost Box) EVP recordings, go to my Yahoo® web site at http://tech.groups.yahoo.com/group/EVP-ITC-SDWR-SpeakingToTheDeadWithRadios-/?yguid=338683728, or you can also listen to others on You Tube® on my channel EVPITCSDWR.

Chapter Three:
The Best Radio

Recently while explaining my Radio Sweep (Ghost Box) EVP process to a friend, he asked me what is the best radio one can use that will work for recording with the dead, and I told him if he had an electronics background he could build his own Radio Sweep (Ghost Box) EVP device like Frank Sumption did, or he could just buy a relatively inexpensive radio from an electronics store and hack it like I did. I further explained that I opted for buying an inexpensive electronics store radio, and used Mike Colleta's hack process on You Tube® to enable it to scan stations un-muted.

This model radio I told him is great for beginners as well as the avid enthusiast and is known as the Shack Hack 12-469 digital scan radio which can be seen at Keyport Paranormal.com, a web site owned and managed by Steve Hultay. Steve has an excellent listing of electronics store radios he has personally hacked and tested communicating with the dead, and listed below are some of these hacked radios with specifics Steve Hultay has provided about each one. You can also see this hacked radio in action on You Tube®, or Google® by searching for Shack Hack 12-469.

Stand-Alone Radios that can be Hacked

Hacking a manufactured radio involves taking apart the radio purchased from an electronics store, for example, and disabling the mute pin, wire or feature which allows the radio to scan or sweep stations un-muted, but you need to know what radios can be hacked before you buy one. The following are a small list of manufactured stand alone radios that can be hacked or altered to work as a Radio Sweep (Ghost Box) EVP device, and you can see them at www.keyportparanormal.com.

Shack Hacks

Shack Hacks are radios purchased from Radio Shack® that have been taken apart and altered by design to work as a Ghost Box.

Radio model 12-469 (White-New Style) is the most popular among Radio Sweep (Ghost Box) EVP enthusiasts. It has AM and FM bands, but requires an external speaker to project the noise as the radio scans or sweeps stations. The type speaker it has is an internal one in which the listener would need ear-buds or stereo head phones. This particular radio, however, is no longer being manufactured, but I have seen some on E-bay for sale with a starting bid price at seventy five dollars. The only complaint I have about this radio is the clicking sound it makes scanning stations on the AM Band. If you have any paranormal messages that need to have the volume raised, the clicking sound is also raised making messages difficult to listen to. I always tell my clients to block out the clicking sound in their mind, so they can hear the recorded messages.

Please note that there is an older radio model 12-469 (Gray and White-Old Style Model) which has the same functions as the newer radio above, but this radio does not have that annoying clicking sound on the AM band. This radio is really hard to find, but if you see one for sale, buy it!

Radio model 12-470 (Gray and White-Old Style Model) has the same features as the model 12-469 radio, but it has a speaker in which the sound of the radio scanning stations can be heard externally. This model radio is also very hard to find. Please note, if you see a model 12-470 for sale that is black, do not buy it since it as it can't be hacked to scan stations un-muted.

Radio model 20-125 has AM/FM and Shortwave and a built in speaker. Steve Hultay of Keyport Paranormal® feels the AM sweeps slowly in his area, but it may work differently for others depending on the strength on the radio signal.

Radio model 12-820 is an armband radio which has AM and FM bands. This
model works pretty well, but like the newer 12-469 radio, you need to buy an external speaker to project the noise of the radio scanning stations. By design, it has an internal speaker which requires ear-buds or stereo head phones to listen to it.

Radio model 12-850 can also be hacked, and it has a speaker complete with the AM and FM bands.

Radio model 12-587 has the AM and FM bands with a speaker, but it is has a manual knob to control the scanning sweep of radio stations.

Radio model 12-588 is a small armband radio that requires an external speaker. This particular radio scans stations or sweeps stations at a decent pace. I recently bought one, and what I like best about this radio is there is no clicking sound on the AM band as there is on the radio model 12-469. I still believe the radio model 12-469 is the best Radio Sweep (Ghost Box) one can use today, that is one can find it, with the 12-588 radio model coming in second.

Wrist Band Radio that can be Hacked

As noted previously, hacking a manufactured radio involves taking apart the radio purchased from an electronics store, for example, and disabling the mute pin, wire or feature which allows the radio to scan or sweep stations un-muted, but you need to know what radios can be hacked before you buy one. The following link displays a wrist band radio that can be hacked or altered to work as a Radio Sweep (Ghost Box) EVP device http://www.insidetheboxrtscghostbox.com/jensensab55hack.html. The first person to hack this Jensen® SAB-55 radio was Bruce Halliday.

Halliday Hack

Bruce Halliday was the first person to successfully hack the Jensen® SAB-55 model radio, and all testing thus far have proven this radio a good match for a beginner. The Halliday Hack, is a manufactured radio by design that comes with AM and FM bands, and while it has an internal speaker in which the user must use ear-buds or stereo head phones to listen to it, an external speaker can be hooked up to it to project the noise of the radio scanning or sweeping stations.

What is important to know about this radio is the model. The model defines whether or not it can be hacked, and sadly I learned the hard way having purchased the radio on-line only to find it was the wrong model that can be hacked. The correct model code you want to make sure this radio has before you buy it must be FA-B. Model codes that can't be hacked are FA-A and FA-C.

This concludes the different types of manufactured radios that can be hacked to work as a Radio Sweep (Ghost Box) EVP device. As a beginner in this field of study, one important piece of advice I have for you is to not go to any electronics store to buy any radio to try and hack it yourself. Save yourself some time and money and contact Steve Hultay of Keyport Paranormal® or Bruce Halliday of Inside the Box RTSC Ghost Box Research to find out what radios they are currently testing and what radios can be hacked to work as a Radio Sweep (Ghost Box) EVP device. Some of these radios can cost upwards to fifty or more dollars, and it would be a shame if you bought one that could not be hacked.

Home Made Radio Sweep (Ghost Box) EVP Radio Devices

A homemade Radio Sweep (Ghost Box) EVP device, I have defined is one in which someone with an electronics background procures radio electronic parts and designs and builds that radio from the ground up.

The following two radio sweep peers I have become acquainted with, Frank Sumption and Joe Cioppi, actually design and build their own homemade radios that are used in conjunction with a digital or a tape recorder to record paranormal messages from the dead. The radios serve as the tool and medium in which the dead somehow use as it scans or sweeps stations and any paranormal messages that occur within the noise of the radio scanning or sweeping the stations are picked up by a tape or digital recorder.

Frank's Box

After testing a young German software engineer's EVP making program, Frank Sumption an American paranormal researcher from Colorado got the idea to create his own EVP device using Radio Sweep technology. By his own design, Frank using spare radio parts from electronics stores built a device that produces random voltage to create raw audio from an AM radio tuner. Raw audio as explained by Frank is comprised of bits of human speech, music and noise, and a good source of raw audio is a radio with its tuning sweeping across the entire bands of AM, FM, or even Short-wave. The sweep can be random, linear, or manual sweep. Within the paranormal community Frank's device goes by two names which are "Frank's Box" or a "Ghost Box". The "Frank's Box", a name coined by Christopher Moon, sweeps across these radio broadcasts producing an endless stream of bits of human speech, music and white noise with the white noise being less important. It is believed that the spirit entities somehow use this raw audio to communicate with us in the form of voices.

Frank's Box Screen Shot (Used with permission of Frank Sumption)

Frank has built several different versions of his radio sweep Ghost Box selling the devices to his peers to test during investigations or personal research. His contributions to this field of study have reached a global level sharing his design plans, personal experiences and guidance with others. As noted in the introduction of this book, Frank Sumption has built over 100 "Frank's Boxes". To learn more about "Frank's Box" you can join Frank Sumption's EVP/ITC Yahoo® web group http://tech.groups.yahoo.com/group/EVP-ITC/?yguid=338683728 . To see additional photographs of a myriad of Franks Boxes, friend me on face book® at http://www.facebook.com/SDWRSpeakingToTheDeadWit hRadios?sk=photos and view my photo album

Joe's Box

Joseph A. Cioppi Sr. a retired engineer from Doylestown, PA was so intrigued by Christopher Moon's demonstration of Frank Sumption's "Frank's Box" on Coast to Coast AM® and on You Tube®, that he acquired a copy of Frank Sumption's Radio Sweep (Ghost Box) design schematics and attempted to build one from the ground up, but stopped when he discovered a Phillips® Electronics FM tuner chip that proved much easier to implement.

This chip had built in features that were more suitable for random selection of radio stations. Just after he successfully bread-boarded a working FM random sweep circuit, he received a call from Steve Hultay, founder of Keyport Paranormal®, who asked Joe to build him a Frank's Box. Joe agreed to do the job, but noted to Steve that had developed a much better design and could package it for Steve while he worked on the Frank's Box build. Hultay mentioned to Joe that he did not believe a slow sweep would be accepted by the skeptics, so Joe changed the timing components to give a wider adjustment range with a faster rate to a slower rate. Hultay also wanted a louder audio output, so his friends could hear the random messages clearly.

Joe's Box Screen Shot (Used with permission of Joe Cioppi)

Early on Joe Cioppi numbered his Radio Sweep (Ghost Box) EVP units which were called "Joe's Box", but he has built so many now that he stopped numbering them. Many of "Joe's Boxes" are now being used within the United States, Scotland, Australia, Mexico, and Canada. All components of this homemade box are built into surplus CB radio shells. To contact or to learn more about Joe Cioppi go to his web site at http://www.freewebs.com/joecioppi/ which is called Philadelphia Spirit Communication.

Electronic Manufacturer Production Model Radio Sweep (Ghost Box) EVP Radio Device

The Spirit Box, Model P-SB7 is the first production Spirit Box device offered to the paranormal community. It is a mini size Spirit Box the size of an MP3 player. The P-SB7 made its premier debut on Ghost Adventures "LIVE" show from the Trans-Allegheny Lunatic Asylum on October 30, 2009 Where the P-SB7 was used by Chris Fleming, a Sensitive, Paranormal Investigator and expert in the Paranormal field. The P-SB7 provided responses to his questions in real time over a 40 minute segment of the show. When used by a properly trained individual, under certain circumstances, the P-SB7 will provide results similar that of an EVP recorder, but in real time. Since then, it has become very popular and can be seen frequently on Ghost Adventures and Psychic Kids where Zak and Chris Fleming continue to receive consistent relevant responses to specific questions.

To learn more about this radio sweep device, or how to purchase it go to http://www.pro-measure.com/P_SB7_SB7_Spirit_Box_s/98.htm

P-SB7 Spirit Box Screen Shot (Used with permission of Gary Galka)

Radio Availability and Design Change Issues

Having presented to you some of the manufactured radios that can be hacked, and homemade radios with photos that are being built from the ground up to work as Radio Sweep (Ghost Box) EVP devices, supplying these radios to everyone in the worldwide market that wants one, is an issue that needs to be resolved.

Through facebook® conversation with some of our Worldwide Radio Sweep – Ghost Box EVP Alliance members who live in other countries outside the United States, some of them have told me they have been unable to find, for example, a Radio Shack® radio in their area to procure. Some of them have even asked some of our USA members to buy and ship them a radio overseas, so they too can hack it and record with their loved ones for messages.

Availability of radios to some people in some countries as noted above is an issue that needs to be resolved as well as another issue in that some of the existing electronics manufacturers that sell the radios we are hacking, are often changing the design of the radio in which some of the design changes make it hard or prevent those hacking radios from finding the correct wire or pin to snip allowing the radio to scan or sweep stations un-muted which makes real time spirit communication possible.

There are three solutions I believe are needed to help ensure anyone in the world who wants to record Radio Sweep (Ghost Box) EVP with their deceased loved ones, with crime victims or missing persons, with spirits during a paranormal investigation, or with any application, and these three solutions are as follows.

Solution 1: Create a Worldwide Radio Sweep (Ghost Box) EVP Community

When I created the Worldwide Radio Sweep – Ghost Box EVP Alliance on facebook®, solution one was introduced. The whole purpose of this group was to bring together everyone involved in Radio Sweep (Ghost Box) EVP together in one place, so we could post recordings, share findings from investigations, share our processes and methods, help newcomers, and to keep all of us abreast of manufactured radios that can be hacked, where you can buy them, as well as share radio design plans with members who have electronic radio background or experience, so they can build their own radios from the ground up.

Solution 2: Inspire Electronic Manufacturers Worldwide to Build and Sell these Devices

As I mentioned previously, one of the issues that hinders our ability to hack radios is the manufacturers often change the design of the radio making it difficult for hackers to locate the pin or wire that can be cut to enable the radio to scan or sweep stations un-muted.

In my opinion, what needs to happen in solution two is we need the electronics manufacturers to build and deploy into production Radio Sweep (Ghost Box) EVP devices, so anyone who has no electronics background that wants to record with their loved ones, can just go out and buy the device.

The ideal candidate, I think, that should build this device selling it in every one of their stores and on-line catalogs worldwide, is Radio Shack®. Their model "white" 12-469 radio which is no longer in production, is the best store bought radio that can be altered and used as a Radio Sweep (Ghost Box) EVP device today! They just need to bring it back, get rid of the clicking noise on the AM band, and market it and sell it as a Ghost Box. Additionally and before they even deploy it into production, they need to let some of us field test it with recommendations as necessary.

Solution 3: Availability Must Be Worldwide

The other issue I had mentioned earlier outside of the manufacturers changing their radio design was some people in countries outside the USA have complained they have not been able to find radios we buy and hack in the United States. Therefore they have tried to get some people in the States to buy and mail them a radio, so they can hack it, and use it.

After solution two is put into motion, and the devices are being manufactured, the electronics manufacturers need to ensure any person in any country can buy one of these radios. If the store that sells them is not situated in their country, then the person should be able to go online to purchase and have the radio shipped to them wherever they live. No person should be deprived of having the ability of buying one of these devices.

The only problem I see after solution two and three are implemented, however is if projected sales of the devices are not met, the manufacturer will likely pull the item and discontinue building them.

What is really key to keeping these Radio Sweep (Ghost Box) EVP devices in production and available at all times, is we need to ensure the devices work, and to ensure they work, some of us especially those with a lot of experience testing and or building this technology from a homemade perspective need to be consulted and given the ability to test prototypes before they are deployed into production. Detailed instruction manuals would also have to be created to teach the person buying the product, how to use it, and what they can use it for other than just trying to contact Uncle Joey who passed away last year. If a device is deployed for sale and it does not work, people are going to return what they bought, and others are not going to buy it.

Have you ever hear this saying "Do you have an app-for that?". This is a common term being said in commercials relative to cell phones. To ensure these Radio

Sweep (Ghost Box) EVP devices should they get mass produced into the worldwide market, do not become a short lived fad like the CB-radio once was, the users or the people that buy them need to know about the many different applications these devices can be used for. For example, one can use the device in conjunction with a tape or preferably a digital recorder to record information from the dead to ask about future and breakthrough technology that companies of today can build and market to the masses. Companies pay big bucks for this information.

In closing this chapter, remember before you go out and buy a radio to try and use it as a Radio Sweep (Ghost Box) EVP device to record messages from the dead, join the Worldwide Radio Sweep Ghost Box EVP Alliance on Face Book and ask members what radios can be hacked http://www.facebook.com/group.php?gid=1021935931789 06&v=wall, or consult with the following two people who currently buy and hack radios. Some of these radios can cost fifty or more dollars, and it would be a shame if you bought one like I did, and it could not be hacked.

Contact Steve Hultay through Keyport Paranormal® at this URL http://www.stevehultay.com/ or contact Bruce Halliday at this URL http://tech.groups.yahoo.com/group/inside_the_box_rtsc_g host_box_research/ to find out which radios can be hacked and where to purchase these radios. These two guys both members of my worldwide group are very talented, and they have many years experience testing and hacking radios, using them to establish communication with the dead.

Chapter Four:
Dark Heads, Demons and Technicians

Before I show you how I personally prepare for and initiate a Radio Sweep (Ghost Box) EVP recording session, I would first like to make you aware what you seek when recording with the dead, you will find. In net if you try and contact an evil spirit, you will, and if you try and contact a nice and loving spirit you will.

A Radio Sweep (Ghost Box) EVP device or even just using a recorder alone is not a device that I condone to be used for evil purposes. Use it to contact your loved ones who have passed on, to run tests where you hold up items in your hands and ask the dead to name the item, or use it as a tool during a paranormal investigation, more importantly use it for something good.

If you use these devices to summon evil entities, you are looking for trouble; you may not be able to get rid of them; and they may very well consume your life bringing unpleasant havoc on you or even your family.

While I envision this book electronically available to readers, for example, on Amazon®, Kindle®, or on the shelves in every book store around the world available in all languages, I expect serious minded adults at least eighteen and over who are interested in learning more about the paranormal or people who are already actively involved in the paranormal to buy and read this book with pure intent to learn and perhaps use these devices and processes to help others.

I do not expect people to use these devices and processes for contacting evil spirits, and I definitely do not recommend these devices be given to or to be used by children under the age of eighteen.

What people need to understand is that the Spirit World is much like the internet, in that you truly do not know who you are talking to which leads us to the next discussion about Dark Heads.

Dark Heads – Negative Entities

Dark Heads, a name coined by Bruce Halliday of Inside the Box RTSC Ghost Box Research on Yahoo®, are negative entities or unfriendly spirits that can interfere with your recording session even if you do not seek them out.

Dark Heads in essence are any spirit that is disruptive or destructive to a Radio Sweep (Ghost Box) EVP session. It feeds on negative energy, and it carries a bad karma and attitude. You can usually detect a Dark Head by the foul language and negative messages and or responses they offer. They will also attempt to deceive you and block any communication between you and the friendly spirits you are engaged in a recording session with, and they are believed to be lower level entities and can usually be stopped or blocked by our friends on the other side, for example your technician, spirit guide, or guardian angel.

On the flip side if you as the researcher are in a bad mood, had an argument with someone or a experienced a bad day at the office and are steeped in negative tension and energy, this will help to reinforce the negative energy of a Dark Head giving them fuel for their fire. The best way to combat these entities is to approach a session only when you have a good attitude and are in a positive frame of mind. These negative entities can enter your recording space and wreak havoc on the recording session itself, sometimes to the point in which the recording session will have to be deleted.

One of my worst experiences with a Dark Head occurred in late 2009 in which the entity consumed about three entire recording sessions with different family clients shouting out the "F-Word" all through each recording session and making threats and comments that I was going to die or be killed or that it was going to get me. I had to delete each of these recordings, and try again on another day, but each time I tried again, the Dark Head was there almost as if it was waiting for me to turn the radio and recorder on.

After about three weeks of this harassment with no solution, I finally confided in a friend who is a Medium, and she suggested I pray to my technician or spirit guide or to God at the beginning of each recording to surround me with white loving light in an effort to keep it away.

About a week later, when I tried to record again using her suggested process, the Dark Head was there again to harass me, but this time while engaged in the recording session, that little voice in my mind told me to leave the radio on and to ask God to make the Dark Head go away and continue with the recording session anyway. Later that day when I listened to what I recorded on playback, and right after I had prayed to God for help, I heard a paranormal message that said "Do not worry. This will never happen again", and sure enough during my next recording, the Dark Head was gone, and has not bothered me since. I personally believe this particular recorded message came from my guardian angel or technician.

While Dark Heads tend to manifest more during Radio Sweep (Ghost Box) EVP recording sessions of inquiry by weekend enthusiast or during a Deceased Loved One, Known Deceased Missing Person or a crime case recording session, other negative entities of the more dangerous type namely demons, tend to manifest and be very troublesome during certain types of paranormal investigations.

Demons – Negative Entities

From a Christian perspective, Demons are evil spirits often associated with possession, and are considered to be minions of Satan. Their whole purpose is to tempt and torment the living leading them to do sinful things, and by definition, Demon means "replete with wisdom".

Demons once attached to a human can suck the life out of a person changing their personal character wreaking uncontrollable havoc which often leads to an exorcism. These are entities you do not want to seek or mess with, and I advise you do not mess with them unless you are expertly qualified, for example a Demonologist, and have been called in by a client to investigate and or assist in exorcising.

Encountering one, however, would more than likely occur during a Paranormal Investigation at a client location in which negative activity is taking place.

The type paranormal investigations I have partaken, not of this type, were arranged though a paranormal meet-up group, organized and managed by professional paranormal investigators who took us into known historic haunted locations free of these issues. Furthermore, these investigators would never take inexperienced people into such locations.

I have, however, been approached by people either through the internet or through the Worldwide Radio Sweep Ghost Box EVP Alliance group on face book® who have asked me to remotely from my home engage a radio sweep recording session with entities they believe are Demons residing in a particular location. In response to such requests, I have responded back that I would not be able to help them. To deal with let alone to record with entities of this type, one must be an experienced professional, again a Demonologist, having knowledge of Demons and how to deal with them.

I strongly advise to any reader of this book if you aren't at least a Demonologist, do not attempt to record Radio Sweep (Ghost Box) EVP with these entities on site or even in the privacy of your home miles away from the location. I am sure you have heard the saying "curiosity killed the cat", and being curious wanting to engage such a recording with no experience under your belt could be the death of you.

Technicians – Positive Helper Entities

Technicians, another paranormal entity coined by Bruce Halliday, are positive entities or spirit guides that are available to assist you during a Radio Sweep (Ghost Box) EVP recording session. Bruce's most notable technicians are Mike and Lisa who have assisted him since he began working with his Radio Sweep (Ghost Box) EVP device to receive live spirit communication. Live spirit communication is another concept as real time spirit communication discussed earlier.

The technician I have is my Guardian Angel whom I have spoken to all my life since I first learned of the guide during Catholic school education.

When I know I am going to record with a deceased client, crime victim or even my father or family members long since passed, I will ask my Guardian Angel to go meet with that deceased person, and ask them to show up in my room at a set time and set day. Usually I will start this process a week ahead of time, and then remind my guide again the night before the recording session.

On the day of the recording, I will ask my technician or guide to envelope the room in white loving light, and help ensure only positive and loving spirits are in my room. I also ask my technician or guide to help ensure only messages from the deceased client show up on my recorder and that they are as clear as possible to be heard with little software amplification.

Having your technician or guide there with you is extremely important, as they are your guardian to help protect you in the event a Dark Head or Demon wanders in to create havoc with your recording.

Technicians – How do you get one?

Having been raised Catholic, I grew up knowing every person has a spirit guide or guardian angel with them at all times, but what about you as the reader. Does your religion or belief system promote the idea of technicians, guardian angels or spirit guides being with you at all times? Even still if they do not, any person can request assistance of a technician or a spirit guide, and all you have to do is pray for one.

Unlike Bruce Halliday who knows the names of his guides Mike and Lisa, I do not know the name of my present guide. When I need help, I just say "Guardian Angel I need your help", and then I tell the angel what assistance I need. My technician or guide is in a sense like my personal assistant when it comes to recording Radio Sweep (Ghost Box) EVP with the dead, and I keep telling the guide that I will have to buy him dinner for an eternity when I die to thank him for all he has done for me.

After reading this book, if you decide to start recording Radio Sweep (Ghost Box) EVP with the dead, I suggest before you first turn your hacked radio and recorder on for the first time, you pray for a technician to help you, and from there each time you want to meet with a deceased person, just ask your technician or guide to help arrange the appointment. Also, after some time, if you wish to know their name, ask for it, and call on them by name going forward.

In closing this chapter, remember to seek out the nice and loving spirits, remember the Dark Heads as they can come about at any time, stay away from recording with a Demon unless you are a Demonologist, and always ensure to call on a Technician, spirit guide or a guardian angel to help assist you and to protect you during your Radio Sweep (Ghost Box) EVP recordings.

Chapter Five:
Preferred Equipment and Making an Appointment to Record with the Dead

In preparation for your first Radio Sweep (Ghost Box) EVP recording with the dead, you obviously will need some equipment, for example, a manual sweep radio, or a hacked digital radio with an external speaker if your model radio has an internal speaker, and a tape or digital recorder.

In this chapter I will teach you the disadvantage in using manual sweep radios verses digital scan, and I will teach you how to make an appointment with the dead to meet for a recording session.

Manual Sweep Radio

For my first Radio Sweep (Ghost Box) EVP recording session with the dead, at that time I only had access to an old manual sweep Worldwide Panasonic® radio, and a Sony® microcassette tape recorder.

Manual sweep is just what it says, which is you turn the radio station sweep dial left or right through the radio stations with your hand fast enough to where you barely hear any announcers with any clarity. During this sweep process you ask questions of the dead with your recorder on and try and capture any paranormal voices that may occur within that noise of the manual scanning or sweeping of stations.

For me two problems arose from using this method and process. One is that my fingers and wrists got very tired trying to turn the dial at the preferred speed while at the same time asking a question, and the second problem that arose involved the tape recorder itself. When using a tape recorder, I found that I could only use that tape one time as just taping another recording over it often allowed sounds from the previous recording to bleed through. Tape recorders when recording EVP, in my personal opinion, are not very reliable and nor are they practical as one would have to keep buying new cassettes for every recording.

During my first manual sweep Radio Sweep (Ghost Box) EVP recording session, I tried to contact my father who passed away in 1987 by asking simple questions like "Daddy are you here?", but I received no response. Later during the recording session, after no success in making contact with my dad, I simply asked "if there are any spirits here with me now, please call out my name". After about ten minutes of sweeping the AM stations manually having heard no responses to my questions, I asked the dead if I should use Short Wave, and I heard real time a message of "Yes!" to which I then switched the band from AM to SW (short wave).

Using short wave when I asked if there were any spirits with me, I immediately received a real time message of "Mike Edwards!"

What is key to know about using manual sweep, is you need to sweep or scan the stations fast enough to not allow too much radio traffic to bleed through where a radio announcer can be heard clearly, but not too fast which presents a problem for the entity to get their message across. Unlike a digital scan radio which does the work for you, turning the radio dial for a manual sweep radio at just the right speed, and every time you record, is tricky at best and not very consistent.

To counter this problem in turning the dial at the right speed and asking your questions at the same time, you may want to have a friend or family member sweep the stations for you, while you ask your questions.

Digital Scan / Sweep Radio

The preferred method for me in recording Radio Sweep (Ghost Box) EVP and the one which I highly recommend is to use a digital scan or sweep radio in conjunction with a digital recorder. When using a digital scan radio, I can scan or sweep the radio stations continuously at the click of a button, and my fingers and wrists do not hurt or get tired. Also by using a digital recorder, I can completely delete every recording with no bleed through issues as experienced using a tape recorder.

As I mentioned earlier, I use a Shack Hack Model 12-469 radio along with a digital recorder. This radio model has an internal speaker, meaning you can only hear stations scanning using ear buds or head phones. Since paranormal messages from the dead show up in the noise of the radio while it scans stations, for this radio you need to project that noise using an external speaker. The speaker jack is plugged into the ear bud/head phone jack on top of the radio.

For this model radio, I personally scan stations using the AM band, mainly due to the fact that fewer stations exist on the AM band in my area than do on the FM band. When there are fewer stations, I have found there appear to be more breaks or blank spots within the noise where paranormal messages often appear for the digital recorder to pickup.

Think of it this way, you are in a room with about fifty people talking, and all you hear is that noise, then all of a sudden everyone stops talking for a second, and you no longer hear the noise of everyone talking. It is within these blank spots as I call them where no radio traffic sounds that paranormal messages often sound off and are picked up by the recorder.

Once you have your equipment ready and operational to record Radio Sweep (Ghost Box) EVP, you are now ready to make an appointment with the dead.

Make an Appointment with the Dead

Making an appointment for a deceased person to meet with you for a Radio Sweep (Ghost Box) EVP recording session or any EVP recording session is very similar to making an appointment for someone to meet you in an office or at your home; however, formal arrangements are not always necessary when recording with the dead, for example, you can just turn the device and recorder on anywhere or at any time to record with the dead.

Most if not all of my recording sessions are engaged through an appointment, and about a week before, as well as on the night before a planned recording session, I will pray to what I call my Guardian Angel or Technician to find the deceased person in the spirit world and ask this angel to have that deceased person or persons to show up in my room the next day at a set time. Depending on your religion, you may have a different name for this contact spirit, but you can also just say a prayer to God or to the deceased person to place this request. Some of my peers have noted that they just say a prayer directly to the deceased, and ask they come the next day. All of the above is fine, but what is important is you somehow let the deceased know you want to meet with them, when, why, and at what time.

It is also important to provide your Guardian Angel as much information you know about the deceased to help ensure the right deceased person shows up. Since we live in a world in which many people can have the same first and last name, providing this additional information is very important.

In 2009, for example, a client asked me to contact her father who recently passed away from cancer. She described him as a gentle loving and kind man, but the spirit that showed up did not fit that description at all. He was not happy to be here, made negative comments about his family, and made negative comments about my ability to hear him.

To combat this problem, I changed my process slightly and now ask the client to also pray to their loved one asking them to come to my home. While there is no guarantee every spirit that comes to my home will indeed be the relative of the client, adding this additional step in the process I believe helps ensure the right contact shows up, but again there is no guarantee.

Chapter Six:
The Recording Session

Whenever I engage a Radio Sweep (Ghost Box) EVP recording session with the dead, I always do it at the same time of day, eight AM, and I almost always record on a Monday. I try to keep this schedule for two reasons, one of which is consistency in that the dead know I will be available on this day and time. The other reason I record to this schedule is because in my area the AM band is not so crowded with radio traffic at this time of day, and having that on my side makes listening to and transcribing any recorded messages much easier.

Before I begin any recording session I start the session with a prayer for protection, and then I introduce myself and lay out the ground rules how I expect the dead to answer me.

Prayer for Protection

While the prayer for protection is debatable by some, I personally believe it is an important first step to help ensure you are protected from negative entities or Dark Heads, entities that can and sometimes do wreak havoc during a recording session. While I have no way to measure the effectiveness of such a prayer, to me just saying it is a security blanket in a sense that it provides me some sense of comfort knowing that God is watching over me while I engage dialog with the dead.

Within the construct of every religion, there are many different prayers one can say, for example, the Hail Mary or the Lord's Prayer both of which I have learned through my Catholic upbringing, and any one is fine. For me, however, I have created the following and very simple prayer which so far has proven effective.

"Almighty God and Jesus please surround today's recording session with white loving light, and please help ensure only positive and loving spirits are with me today"

Introduction with Ground Rules

Prior to turning the recorder and the radio on for all session types, I always introduce myself and explain what I plan to do, that I cannot see or hear them, and I also explain how they should answer me. For example, I will ask them to wait until after I have asked the question before they answer me; I will explain that I will only allow them ten to fifteen seconds to answer each question, and at the end of the ten or fifteen seconds, I further explain when they hear me say the word OK, that means I am about to start asking my next question.

All of the above is very important as I have found

during playback of some recordings, the dead often make comments like "Why is he not looking at me? Why is he not answering me?", or they talk when I am asking them a question which makes it hard for me to understand what they said over my voice.

After the prayer has been said, and the introduction and the ground rules have been explained, I will start the recording session first by turning on the recorder in record mode, and then set the radio to scan the AM band.

Turning the recorder on in record mode first is very important to help ensure you do not miss any instant messages that can and often do occur when you turn the radio on in scan mode. If the recorder is not on in record mode, and a real time paranormal message sounds, you will miss recording it, and just have another fish tale to tell others about what you heard but missed.

Within this chapter, I have outlined four different types of Radio Sweep (Ghost Box) EVP recording sessions I personally engage in the first one being the best for beginners.

1. Show and They Tell

2. Deceased Loved One

3. Known Deceased Missing Person

4. Paranormal Investigations

Show and They Tell

For a beginner the easiest way to learn how to record Radio Sweep (Ghost Box) EVP and to recognize or discern any Paranormal voice messages, is to engage in what I call a "Show and They Tell" recording session. This is the method I actually used to learn the process of recording, listening to and transcribing what I heard.

For this type of recording session, I follow the same process as noted above by making an appointment with a deceased or deceased spirits, and after I say my prayer, introduce myself and lay out my ground rules, set the recorder to record mode and turn the radio on setting it to scan or sweep stations, I hold up items in my hand and ask any dead in my room to tell me the name of the item. Below is how a typical "Show and They Tell" recording session is engaged.

Engage the "Show and They Tell" Recording Session

"Almighty God and Jesus please surround today's recording session with white loving light, and please help ensure only positive and loving spirits are with me today".

Good morning. My name is Michael Edwards, and I am hoping there are some kind and loving deceased spirits here with me today. As you can see laid out before me, I have a radio with an external speaker and a digital recorder. Today I will try to record any messages from you when I hold up some items for you to name using a process known as Radio Sweep (Ghost Box) Electronic Voice Phenomena. The design of this radio has been altered to ensure it scans radio stations continuously not muted, and it is believed that somehow when you talk to me from the spirit world, you somehow assemble words from the radio traffic into meaningful short phrases or sentences, messages I may hear real time or on play back. When I turn this recorder and radio on, I will ask you some questions. Please do not speak on your end until after I have asked my question, and when you hear me say the work OK, that means I will ask you another question".

After this announcement to the deceased present in my room, I turn the recorder on setting it to record mode, then turn the radio on at high volume, set it to scan continuously, and then I will place the recorder about a fist length away from the external speaker, and start asking questions.

During my first "Show and They Tell" Radio Sweep (Ghost Box) EVP recording session, I held up a carved wooden dolphin I had completed earlier in the week, and I asked any deceased in my room to tell me what kind of animal it was that I had carved. I received several responses of the word "Fish", and then two loud responses of the word "Dolphin". The words Fish, I heard later on play back, but the two words of "Dolphin" I heard real time during the recording session, and I was able to respond to them that I heard what they said.

You can listen to this actual recording session on You Tube® at this link using head phones. http://www.youtube.com/watch?v=hLEksaxD1so&list=UU c2D5p1G0G_IZer1LTswYEw&index=30&feature=plcp

During this same recording session, I also held up a watch, a stapler, eye glasses, a pencil, a wooden sail boat, scissors, and a telephone each to which I received accurate responses, some real time, and some heard later on playback of the digital recorder.

What I found interesting about some of my recording sessions using the "Show and They Tell" method is during some recording sessions, not all the items were accurately named. I began to wonder that perhaps some of the dead here in my house were from different historical timeframes, and obviously would not know the difference between a traditional phone, a cell phone or a digital recorder.

For example, during one of my "Show and They Tell" recordings, I held up a digital recorder, and received a message of phone, and in another recording session when I held up a remote control for my TV, I got a message of "cell phone". When you as the reader engage in the "Show and They Tell" method, try everything you can think of to show them, and if you have old antiques, holding up those items to be named should be an interesting session as well.

What makes using the "Show and They Tell" Radio Sweep (Ghost Box) EVP recording method an excellent starting point for beginners, is that it is fun, and the questions and answers are short, and are easier to listen for on playback. When you hear this type of messages real time, that my friend is the icing on the cake!

To listen to all of my "Show and They Tell" recordings, go to my Yahoo® web group at this address, and click on Files. http://tech.groups.yahoo.com/group/EVP-ITC-SDWR-SpeakingToTheDeadWithRadios-/?yguid=338683728

Deceased Loved One

A deceased loved one Radio Sweep (Ghost Box) EVP recording session is one in which you contact either your deceased family member or a client's deceased family member to try and record messages to get back to the family.

For this type of recording session, I initially engage

the recording process in the same manner as I would the "Show and They Tell" recording session, first by setting up the appointment with the deceased through my guide, God, or directly with the deceased. Next and on the day and hour of the recording I will initiate my opening prayer for a good session and protection. Then after the opening statement, in which I introduce myself and lay out the ground rules, I will begin the session.

After this announcement to the deceased present in my room, I will turn the recorder on setting it to record mode, turn the radio on at high volume and set it to scan continuously, and then I will place the recorder about a fist length away from the external speaker, and start asking questions.

Below I have outlined two different scenarios, one being a recording with my father, and the other a recording with a client's loved one.

Recording session with my Dad:

1. Daddy, are you here? (I wait ten seconds, and say the word OK).

2. Daddy if you are here, please tells me what you want me to know. (I wait fifteen to twenty seconds, and say the word OK).

3. Daddy I am getting ready to shut down now. If you have anything else to say to me, please say it now. (I wait fifteen to twenty seconds, and say the word OK).

4. Daddy I am shutting down now. I love you! Goodbye!

Typical recording session with a client's deceased loved one:

1. Hello is Jane Doe here today? (I wait ten seconds, and say the word OK).

2. Jane if you are here, do you have a message for your sister Karen? (I wait fifteen to twenty seconds, and say the word OK).

3. Jane who met you when you crossed over into Heaven? (I wait fifteen to twenty seconds, and say the word OK).

4. Jane is your mother Emily with you today? (I wait ten seconds, and say the word OK).

5. If Emily Doe is here today does she have a message for her husband Charles? (I wait fifteen to twenty seconds, and say the word OK).

6. Jane I am getting ready to shut down now. If you have anything else to say to your sister Karen, please say it now. (I wait fifteen to twenty seconds, and say the word OK).

7. Jane I am shutting down now. God bless you! Goodbye!

Recording with my dad is quite different than recording with a client in that I just ask him to tell me what he wants me to know. Early on I starting asking my dad specific questions about where he was, and what is it like there, but he never answered them. He just tells me what he wants me to know.

When recording with a client's deceased loved one, I follow the same path as dad's recording from a process perspective, but I generally ask more questions about the crossing over, who met them, who is there with them now, and I also ask any additional questions the client wants to know.

During most if not all client recordings, I will ask other questions outside what the client asked me to, and sometimes mysterious thoughts pop into my head to ask certain questions. It is almost like the dead are communicating to me telepathically to ask them a certain question.

For example, during one recording session with a friend's mother, I received a thought in my mind to ask about her dog that never liked me, and she provided me information about the dog to which the client was able to validate. In that same recording, she also made a comment about her son eating candy. My friend is a diabetic, and he told me unknown to his family, he has a hidden stash of candy at work that obviously his dead mother was alluding to.

Another good example, in which a thought came through, occurred during a recording with a woman's brother who recently passed. My intention was to just record with him, but during the recording session, I received a thought in my mind to ask if his dad was with him. Thereon I proceeded to ask his dad if he had a message for his wife, to which he gave several messages.

If you have never recorded with any decease relative using either a radio sweep device or even just a tape or digital recorder, some responses may shock you as they did me the first time recording. My thought coming into this process was for every recording with my father or relative or friend or client that all messages received would be loving and wonderful.

At the time I had this vision of heaven being a place where everyone was happy and everyone loved and was happy with everyone there and here as well on earth, but what I found is many deceased individuals provide negative responses about the goings on in the physical world they are not happy with. Some even complain how their estate was divided up, how children or grand children are being raised, or they even complain about what they hear others in the physical world saying about each other. I found, more especially through recording with my father, that the dead can see and hear everything going on here. God knows when we are naughty or nice, and so do our loved ones know when we are naughty or nice. To those of you that believed in Santa Clause as a child, their knowing follows the same concept as Santa knowing if you have been naughty or nice.

So where am I going with this dialog, you may ask? After reading this book, should you make the decision to procure and hack a radio, get a recorder and start recording with a Deceased Loved One, you should expect to receive both positive and negative messages, negative if the dead are unhappy with what you are doing or not doing in the physical world. You should not expect as did I that every message is going to be peachy keen and wonderful with great praise. If you are messing up, you will be told. If you are doing great, you will get praise, and if you are doing badly you will be scolded.

Remember I told you previously it took me several months before I finally made contact with my father, but during that time, I was recording for clients, trying to make contact with their loved ones to relay back messages to them. It was through these recordings with clients that I learned my vision of heaven was not totally correct, and I was often faced with a dilemma in that I had to decide should I make the client aware of the negative messages, or just give them the good stuff. Just give them the good stuff is something I learned about many years ago when I used to pay psychics and mediums cash money for a reading, the reader would actually ask me if I wanted to hear the bad stuff too or only the good stuff. This was a difficult choice I had to make with clients, but since I wanted to be honest in what I had recorded, I to this day always inform the client of any negative messages received, before handing over the goods. For those clients that tell me nope that is not something my family member would say, I just give them the good stuff, and for those that say they want it all, I give them all the messages recorded.

Reading what I just said that some clients said they want it all, how do you the reader think they reacted when they got the material? Some were completely devastated and focused completely on the negative recorded messages ignoring all the good stuff, but some recognized the validity of the negative messages, or ignored the negative messages, and cherished the good stuff even to this day.

Think about this. If you the reader of this book record a negative message with a deceased client, and the living client says they do not understand it, or they say it is not true or that it does not relate to their family at all, you may wonder where did the message come from? It could be that this message is radio traffic; it could be a Dark Head giving you false information; it could be another deceased spirit watching the recording session speaking to another while the session is taking place, or it could also be valid, perhaps a message the client does not remember or is not even aware of. What is very key is when you record for a client you the recorder should not discern the meaning of the message. The client is the person that by listening to the message should determine if the message has any meaning to them.

So we talked about negative messages that can occur during a Radio Sweep (Ghost Box) EVP recording session, what about positive or neutral messages received, ones in which the client has no clue what they mean? Again, we as the recorder in my personal opinion can't nor should we ever discern any message that is recorded for a client. The client is the one who determines if this message has meaning.

Not long ago I recorded for one of my workmates, recording with her mother long since passed. When I asked the deceased mother to give messages about the client's children whom she never saw as they were born after she had passed, I recorded a message that went something like this " Paul got in trouble for saying a girl had big boobs"

The client told me this message had no meaning to her, but later she got back in touch with me as she remembered in Kindergarten her son did get in trouble for making comments about a classmates breasts. Paul is her son's middle name, but he is never called by that name by the living family.

During another recording session, but with a crime victim, the deceased teen kept saying what sounded like CRX. This was a repeatable message through many recording sessions, and I was thinking maybe it had something to do with his being murdered. After some time, the advocate I was working with shared this information with one of the teen's relatives, in fact the teen's relative that had asked the advocate to get involved in the case, and the relative said she knew exactly what CRX was. She had a Honda model CRX automobile, and her nephew always teased her about her CRX in comparison to his hot rod much faster car.

In another recording session with a missing teen, when I asked if he had a message for his mother, and he said "Hearts". Hearts means nothing to me, but to their relative it has meaning.

Before I end this discussion on recording with a Deceased Loved One, I want to make you all aware that not always will you be successful at making contact with the dead person or persons you made an appointment with. Unlike the Show and They Tell recording session in which you can make an appointment or you can just turn the devices on and record with any dead that happen to be present in your home, related to you or not, the deceased you invited through an appointment may not show up at all.

I remember when I first tried to contact my father starting in February of 2008, but for some unknown reason I did not make contact with him until October 2008. I made contact with other deceased using the Show and They Tell recording process as well as contact with Known Deceased Missing Persons, but not with my father.

It was a big mystery at the time, and I remember discussing this with my wife just after I finally did make contact with my father. My wife posed this question to me "If you made contact with your father in February 2008, do you think you would have gotten involved recording with recording Radio Sweep (Ghost Box) EVP with deceased missing children?" My response was that I probably would not have gotten involved as I would have focused all my efforts on recording with my father.

My primary focus at that time was to try and make contact with my father, and when I could not, I continued recording with the dead in my home. Through posting the results from my Show and They Tell recording sessions on Steve Hultay and Frank Sumption's EVP-ITC Yahoo® groups, I met Juli Velasquez who got me involved with missing children cold case files. Perhaps in my father's case in which contact was delayed, this delay was meant to happen.

Another example of not making contact involved my trying to contact a person that committed suicide, and the response I received was "He aint here", and in yet another recording session with a deceased person that was supposed to be a kind and loving father of a client, the deceased person that showed up was very angry, and whoever he was, he was very belligerent. All he did was complain about my asking him to come to my home, and made negative comments about my ability to hear him. When I discussed my results with the client, she said without a doubt this deceased person in the recording was not her father. My only thought was perhaps he was another man with the same first and last name that had arrived or perhaps he was a Dark Head.

From this experience, I changed my process slightly, and I now ask the client to also pray to their loved one to ask them to come to my home for a recording session in addition to my asking my Guardian Angel to set up the appointment with the deceased.

One year later, when this same client asked me to try to contact her kind and loving father again, I finally made contact, and indeed her father was a kind and loving man which made for a wonderful recording experience.

Known Deceased Missing Person

For a known deceased missing person Radio Sweep (Ghost Box) EVP recording session I initially engage the recording process in the same manner as I would the "Show and They Tell" recording session following all steps prior to engage.

Below I have outlined a typical "Known Deceased Missing Person" recording session.

Recording session with missing teen John Doe:

1. John Doe are you here? (I wait ten seconds, and say the word OK)

2. John Doe if you are here, please tell the police what happened to you. (I wait fifteen to twenty seconds, and say the word OK)
3. John Doe did you know the people that fought with you at the gas station? (I wait fifteen to twenty seconds, and say the word OK)
4. John Doe who was chasing you down the highway? (I wait fifteen to twenty seconds, and say the word OK)
5. John Doe I am shutting down now. Thanks for coming. God bless you! Goodbye!

Recording with crime victims, I must tell you can be quite disturbing. The deceased victims will tell you all the gruesome details of what happened to them, many of which can bring you to tears just listening to it.

One child, for example, told me how he walked in on his step mother and another man having relations, and that man stabbed him to death, and disposed of his body before his father came home from a business trip. This boy's body has yet to be found.

In another missing person case recording a young adult, he told me he was taken from a bar, tied up and placed in the trunk of a car filled with dead raccoons, and the car was sunk in a lake. Like before this victim's body has yet to be found.

Not all missing person or crime cases, however, are gruesome from a recording perspective.

Not long ago I was approached to record with a man believed to have fallen through the ice while walking his dog. When I recorded with him, he told me his body was by the bridge stuck under water. Due to the river being mostly frozen over, police had to wait until it thawed to resume their search. When they resumed their search, they found his body by the bridge.

In another recording involving a missing twenty year old single mother with a young son, who was eventually found having drowned in a canal lock, her relative asked me to continue recording with the girl to ask her who in the family she wanted to raise her son. Due to an approaching custody hearing, her relatives wanted to ensure her son was taken in by someone she wanted. The young deceased girl gave me the name of the family she wanted to raise her son, and the client knew exactly who they were and relayed the message.

In Chapter Twelve, I will discuss in more detail actual recording sessions of this type providing recommendations.

Paranormal Investigations

Recording Radio Sweep (Ghost Box) Electronic Voice Phenomena during a paranormal investigation follows a much different path than the three recording session types just mentioned. While an appointment is made with the dead who reside where the paranormal investigation is taking place, the recording session will usually involve more than one person, and can be initiated inside more than one room or outside location at the residence or facility the investigation takes place.

The more people involved with this type of recording session brings to the table more issues to deal with in terms of asking the question and allowing time for an answer, and then asking the next question, and so on.

For example, when recording in your home or somewhere by yourself, or even in a room with a client present, you are in complete control of the recording session, but when you record with a group of people some people may start talking or make a noise when the question is being asked or make a noise during the time you have allotted the dead to answer, and this causes issues when you listen to the recording on playback to transcribe any Suspect or Paranormal messages.

If you plan to use a Radio Sweep (Ghost Box) EVP device during a paranormal investigation, and unless you manage and run this group yourself, you should always ask permission to use it. I belong to a local paranormal meet-up group, and not always do they allow me to bring and use my device. You should always ask for permission first otherwise you may offend a member of that group that does not like or is not in agreement with using Radio Sweep (Ghost Box) EVP devices during an investigation.

Some people I have met that engage in paranormal investigations may have mediumistic abilities, or even may be a sensitive. Sitting in a room with a person playing a noisy Radio Sweep (Ghost Box) EVP device, I was told increases the stress level of some of these individuals having to listen to all the noise from the radio scanning stations, and while the radio sweep recorder may be able to hear the dead, these individuals can't.

I have also learned even if we took turns, allowing the medium and or sensitive to listen, record and use their skills for a set period of time, and then I am given some time to use my radio sweep device for a set period of time, the medium and or sensitive continued to get stressed out over the noise.

My recommendation to a paranormal investigation group that want to include Radio Sweep (Ghost Box) EVP devices as part of their tool set, is to develop an investigation process which would consist of two teams to enter the client location, but each separately.

Team one would consist of people with recorders and cameras who have medium, and or sensitive skills, and team two would consist of people with Radio Sweep (Ghost Box) EVP devices with recorders and cameras.

Imagine a fictional location that is a one story ranch home in which a family who has been living in the home for decades, just recently started to experience hearing voices and seeing spirits in the house. In this fictional home contractors renovating the master bedroom are experiencing objects being thrown at them while working, and regardless of the activity, they continue to show up for work every day.

As a paranormal investigator, I am sure your first thought is the dead are unhappy with the master bedroom being renovated. You have seen this happen before as have other paranormal investigators.

To try and understand what the problem is, I

recommend you send in team one, the medium and or sensitive group to enter each room in the house to ask questions, record for any response messages, and to take pictures all the while trying to see, sense and communicate with the spirits in the home. In this fictional home, when the medium and or sensitive get to the master bedroom, they sense and record an angry spirit shouting at them, but they do not understand what this angry spirit is saying when they hear the messages on play back after leaving the home. Note what I just said which is that they listened to the messages on play back after they left the home.

Next the group leader sends in team two, but instructs them to go directly to the master bedroom to start asking questions recording using their Radio Sweep (Ghost Box) EVP device and recorder.

Imagine team two's leader asks the angry spirit why they are mad, and imagine they hear a real time response that says "mad at Paul!". OK says the team two leader, can you tell me who Paul is? The angry spirit responds real time "worker". Hearing the word "worker" real time from the angry spirit, the team two leader asks the angry spirit why he is mad at Paul, and they do not hear anything, and for some unknown reason all communication stops.

After team two leaves the house, and they listen to what they recorded on play back just after asking the angry spirit why it was mad at Paul, they hear a lower sounding response message of "he is stealing beer". This response message was not heard real time, but could be heard with head phones on play back.

If you are a paranormal investigator reading this book, and if you bought this book to learn what Radio Sweep (Ghost Box) EVP is all about thinking perhaps it may prove a valuable new discovery tool for your investigators, from reading the fictional investigation I just described to you, do you see how this tool and process can help you better understand what is really going on at a location, once the medium or sensitive identifies the problem spirit and or the area at the location with the most activity? Furthermore can you see by my example how you can introduce radio sweep devices into your existing process and not upset or turn off the medium or sensitive group members by separating these investigators who each have very unique skills into two different teams?

In my opinion, if you add this tool and process to your arsenal, and if the conditions are right for real time spirit communication enabling you to engage a two way conversation with the dead hearing response messages to your questions, doing so will enable you to ask more questions while you and your team try and understand what is going on.

Just using the traditional recorder only process to me is not enough, and by adding a Radio Sweep (Ghost Box) EVP device to your list of tools, I believe doing so will help facilitate your investigation process helping to reduce your number of repeat visits.

Chapter Seven:
Upload and File Conversion

Within this chapter I have outlined the process I personally use to upload and convert recorded files from my digital recorder to a wave file.

Before I upload my recorder ".WMA" file to my computer, I set up a folder on my computer. Let us imagine this is a brand new case, so for each new case, I will set up a folder called "Jane Doe", then in that folder I will set up a sub-folder called "Jane Doe June 6 2008", and for every recording going forward with this case, I will create a new sub folder in the same format.

For the purposes of this instruction, I will proceed to outline next steps using a digital recorder, and this recorder is equipped with a cable to upload the ".WMA" file from the recorder to a folder on my computer.

Note above I have already created a folder called Jane Doe, and a sub-folder called Jane Doe June 6 2008. To help ensure the file is not corrupted, you need to ensure the recorder is set in the off position. Next I pull the sleeve off as noted in my manual, and plug in the cable, and then plug that cable into the computer. A ping will announce on your computer, and from here you follow the instructions per your model computer and move or drag the ".WMA" file to the sub folder.

Please note the below screen shots may not apply to your digital recorder upload instructions, but they should give you a good idea how the process works.

For example, see below.

1. I create a main folder.

 Jane Doe

2. I upload my recorded file per the recorder manual instructions

Screen Shot (Used with permission of Microsoft®)

3. I click on the Open Folder to view files, and click OK. Note your computer may be different.

4. For my recorder, I open folder DSS_FLDA which is where the wma file is. Please you the reader of this book should read your recorder upload process to determine how to upload your recording to your computer

5. I ensure that sub-folder Jane Doe June 6 2008 is open, and drag the ".WMA" file into the folder.

6. See below it now sits in the sub-folder

Screen Shot (Used with permission of Microsoft®)

7. The next step in the process is to change the ".WMA" file into a ".WAV" file

    I use an awesome software program called Switch NCH Swift Sound Software®, and you can go to the web and get a download. http://www.nch.com.au/switch/index.html. The version I use is V1.05.

8. Inside NCH Switch®, I press add file as below to capture the ".WMA" file from the sub-folder

Upper Left Screen Shot (Used with permission of NCH Swift Sound Software® Version 1.05) *Lower Right Screen Shot* (Used with permission of Microsoft®)

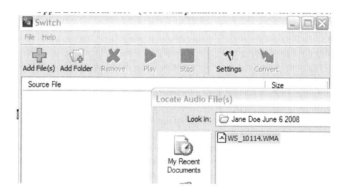

9. Once the file is added, I set the output format to ".wav", and set the output folder to the sub-folder. You need to ensure you redo the output folder every time as you will/can add the newly converted file into the wrong sub-folder.

Screen Shot (Used with permission of NCH Swift Sound Software® Version 1.05)

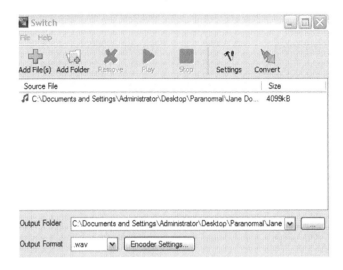

10. Next I press the convert button

Doing so, converts the file.

Note below, that you still have the original ".WMA" file and the new ".wav" files in your sub folder.

Screen Shot (Used with permission of Microsoft®)

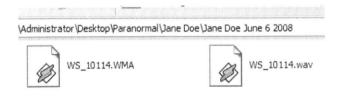

Chapter Eight:
File Segmentation and De-noise

After the Radio Sweep (Ghost Box) EVP recording has been uploaded to the computer and converted to a wave file, the next step in my process is to segment or split out each question with answer saving each into its own wave file, and de-noise only if absolutely necessary.

This process I am about to teach you, the file segmentation and de-noise process is the first of multiple steps in my process to get the wave files ready to be transcribed into a Microsoft® Excel worksheet, so the client or even you the reader can review what was recorded and try to discern what all these recorded messages mean. Further segmentation in which you break these files into smaller units will come later on in the process when I start to listen to and actually begin to transcribe them.

File Segmentation

To segment each file, I use an audio editing software program called Free Audio Editor®

http://www.free-audio-editor.com/index.htm 2009 Version 6.0.1

The reason I split these questions with answer files up saving them each into their own wave file is because it is much easier to listen to rather than trying to listen to the entire file all at once. I have found the response messages appear to be compressed if they are all in one file.

To better explain what I mean by the response messages being compressed, imagine a wide rubber band all stretched out, and if you write a bunch of words and sentences on it, and release it, all you see are a bunch of letters and maybe you might be able to make out one or more words. If you stretch it out, you can read all the words. Therefore, if I have five questions with answers from the dead recorded all in one wave file, I have noticed that a lot of the words in those recorded messages are compressed to the point where if you listened to them, you would not be able to understand them. I first noticed this when I first started recording crime and family cases in which I would ask long questions and allow ten to fifteen seconds for the dead to answer the questions.

Playing around with Free Audio Editor® I would block off sections of messages in the file to try and listen to them, and found the real time messages being the loudest stood out, but the other messages before and after the real time messages were hard to hear.

I also noticed I could not understand some of my questions as they appeared to be compressed as well. This was a rare occurrence, but when I heard it, that is what really got me to thinking, what if I separate each of the five questions I asked in, for example, in a five minute recording session, and then save them in their own wave file.

I did that, and I noticed the messages that occurred after I asked the question, even the lower sounding messages that occurred before and after any real time messages, were now heard more clearly.

Playing around with these files even more, I found if I split each question with answer file up into multiple wave files, that action seemed to open up, un-compress those word messages even more to where they could be heard more clearly. The way these messages came to me that were picked up on that recorder seemed to be arranged in a sliver format like hundreds of Pringle® potato chips all crammed into one can. The can in a sense was the five minute recording session.

Open the Wave File

To segment the converted wave file, I open Free Audio Editor® and in the left navigator I click Open File and browse for my ".wav" file WS_10114.wav inside sub-folder Jane Doe June 6 2008, and open it up.

What I am about to show you is my personal method for file segmentation, but you may feel it necessary to devise your own.

Next, I click Save File as and rename the ".wav" file, for example, to Jane Doe June 6 2008, and thereafter, I rename it again to TEST Jane Doe June 6 2008.

It is the TEST file that I will use to do my segmentation, and when complete, I will just delete what remains of that file.

Next I create a new folder called RAW (unedited original file folder), and I drag the original recording Jane Doe June 6 2008 into that folder.

Now that I have TEST Jane Doe June 6 2008 open, I open it up and start to listen to each question and answer, and at the end of each answer, I stop the recording where I want to segment, and I use my mouse pointer and block off all audio to the right of the first question with answer and delete it.

Screen Shot (Used with permission of Free Audio Editor® 2009 Version 6.0.1)

After I have deleted all audio to the right, I will then click Save File as Jane Doe 1 June 6 2008.

Screen Shot (Used with permission of Free Audio Editor® 2009 Version 6.0.1)

With the first question with answer file now saved, I edit out the remaining four questions with answers and save them each into their own file but in the order in which they were recorded.

Below is an example of what I should have after I have segmented the main TEST file into smaller segments..

Sub-folder Jane Doe June 6 2008 should have a folder named RAW which will include the original recording session named Jane Doe June 6 2008, and each of the segmented question and answer files for questions one, two, three, four, and five.

Sub-folder Jane Doe June 6 2008

RAW (Folder) Jane Doe June 6 2008

- Jane Doe 1 June 6 2008
- Jane Doe 2 June 6 2008
- Jane Doe 3 June 6 2008
- Jane Doe 4 June 6 2008
- Jane Doe 5 June 6 2008

De-noise files for Transcription

In the event any of the files I have segmented have a lot of static or background noise, to better hear those paranormal messages, I may need to de-noise them. Beware, however, that de-noising a file, can degrade the quality of a paranormal message, and I recommend you use this process below only when necessary

I personally use an awesome de-noise program called Clear Voice® which can be purchased on the web for about $50.00.

Clear Voice® is a software product from the Speech Technology Center® http://speechpro.com/ . There is a newer more advanced de-noiser that can be seen here http://speechpro.com/product/analysis-noise/denoiserbox

After you have downloaded Clear Voice®, open up the program, and press the Load Source button to load the noisy file from Jane Doe June 6 2008 sub-folder, file Jane Doe 1 June 6 2008.

- Jane Doe 1 June 6 2008
- Jane Doe 2 June 6 2008
- Jane Doe 3 June 6 2008
- Jane Doe 4 June 6 2008
- Jane Doe 5 June 6 2008

Next set the Noise Reduction Degree to 1 (soft) – 8 db. For me this provides the best reduction in noise, so I can hear the recorded voices with good clarity.

Screen Shot (Used with permission of Speech Technology Center®)

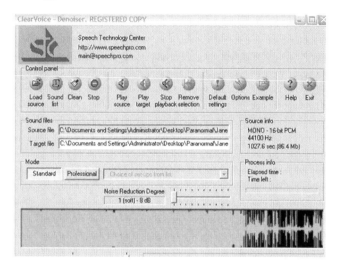

Next, I press the clean button, and after the file is cleaned, it will be named and saved as Jane Doe 1 June 6 2008_CLR.wav.

The cleaned file or de-noised file is the file that I want to use in transcription, and not the original segmented file or file which exhibits the noise.

When the noisy file has been cleaned twice, the files within this folder will be displayed as below.

✓ Please note that within my process, I clean all noisy files once, and each time a file is cleaned, it gets an added extension of "_CLR".

Jane Doe 1 June 6 2008

Jane Doe 1 June 6 2008_CLR

Jane Doe 1 June 6 2008_CLR_CLR

- Jane Doe 2 June 6 2008
- Jane Doe 3 June 6 2008
- Jane Doe 4 June 6 2008
- Jane Doe 5 June 6 2008

Next I will delete the file that displays the file ending of (_CLR) to the recycle bin, and then move the original segmented file into the folder I created named RAW. I do this for two reasons, one being if for any reason, I error on editing the cleaned file, I can always go back to original files in the RAW folder, and then clean it again with Clear Voice®. The second reason is if the client wants to listen to the complete question with answer file after I have cleaned and segmented it further into smaller more manageable files, they can.

Chapter Nine:
Classifying Radio Traffic, Suspect Paranormal, and Paranormal Messages

Chapter Nine is the most important chapter in this book. If you skip any chapters in this book, do not skip this one.

Teaching anyone how to listen for and transcribe Radio Sweep (Ghost Box) EVP messages is not an easy process mainly due to the fact these paranormal messages occur and are mixed in with the Radio Traffic. To truly hear them all, both loud and faint, they need to be isolated or to be more precise, they need to be dissected and saved into their own wave files in the order in which they were recorded. As noted in the introduction of this book, Radio Sweep (Ghost Box) EVP are believed to be messages from the dead that show up in the noise, the raw audio of the radio scanning stations, and these words which can be male, female, young or old sounding, animated or even electronic sounding are believed to be somehow assembled by the dead from the radio traffic into intelligible messages often in one or more words, short phrases or longer sentences and often real time.

What I am about to explain to you is my own personal process one of which may or may not relate to processes used by my peers or mentors. In no way am I dictating to you as the reader that my process is the best or better than another's. I learned Radio Sweep (Ghost Box) EVP from others and thereon tweaked what I was taught into a process that works for me. Think of my process as a starting point from which you too can tweak to best fit your needs, and please understand since Radio Sweep (Ghost Box) EVP is an evolving process, your personal process may change many times as has mine.

What I find unique about my process as compared to that of my peers and mentors, is that I segment the recording into smaller more manageable units, and I isolate each paranormal message into their own wave file rather than keep the entire file whole.

One of the most common questions I get asked by friends, acquaintances, or newcomers interested in learning Radio Sweep (Ghost Box) EVP is how do I personally determine if the recorded voices I have on my recorder are Radio Traffic verses Suspect Paranormal. This is a valid question to ask, and one of the most difficult to answer.

Through much recording, listening to and analysis of my Radio Sweep (Ghost Box) EVP recordings, using the Shack Hack 12-469 radio on the AM band , I have noticed three very distinct voice types that appear to be the norm which are the squeaky mouse sounding voices, the hoarse sounding voices, and the whisper sounding voices. There is a fourth voice type which occurs quite infrequently, and this voice is the human sounding voices which are often confused with being Radio Traffic.

In this chapter I will teach you how I personally try and determine if Radio Sweep (Ghost Box) EVP voice audio messages are Radio Traffic, Suspect Paranormal or Paranormal.

Radio Traffic Audio Voices

Since this book is about Radio Sweep (Ghost Box) Electronic Voice Phenomena, and since a radio is used as part of the recording process, Radio Traffic which I define as the voices of radio announcers will show up in your recorded wave files on play back. There is no getting around this, so expect it.

When I record with the dead, whether it is a Show and They Tell, Deceased Loved One, Known Deceased Missing Person, or even a Paranormal Investigation, I work to isolate and reveal what I call recorded Suspect Paranormal and through validation the Paranormal voice audio messages from the deceased to the living client.

To discern or identify Radio Traffic audio voices within a Show and They Tell recording session, if I hold up a carved wooden dolphin, and I ask the dead in my room to name the animal, and I hear the following voice messages occur just after I ask my question"1610 top forty, fish, Obama said, fish, fish, North Carolina, dolphin, dolphin", I would deem the voice audio messages of "1610 top forty, Obama said, North Carolina" as classic Radio Traffic. Likewise in a Deceased Loved One recording session if I am recording with my father, and I ask my dad if he has any messages for me, and I record voice messages that say "Duke basketball, (?), I saw you carving, (?), today, (?), Wake County", I would deem "Duke basketball, Wake

Country" also as Radio Traffic.

I would also follow the same process of identification when listening to a Known Deceased Missing Person or a Paranormal Investigation recording session to identify the Radio Traffic which generally speaking is easy to identify because based on all recordings I have engaged in thus far, these voices tend to always sound human, and not of the voice type of the squeaky mouse, hoarse, and whisper sounding voice audio messages.

While it is true per our learning and experience that some human sounding voices are indeed messages from the dead, most explicitly human sounding voices I have found to be radio traffic.

The following outlines how I personally identify Radio Traffic in my segmented Radio Sweep (Ghost Box) EVP audio messages.

Identify Radio Traffic

To explain how I identify Radio Traffic in each question with answer file, and thereon isolate and save each Suspect Paranormal or through validation save the Paranormal audio voice messages from the dead, let's take the first question with answer file Jane Doe 1 June 6 2008, and for purposes of this example, let's say this file asks the question "Jane Doe who met you when you crossed over?". Since this is a question with answer file, working to my process, I will listen to the file, and slice or further segment the file into smaller units listening to where a message in the form of a sentence begins and ends.

Just after I ask the question Jane Doe who met you when you crossed over, I hear audio that says "1610 top forty, dad met me, Raleigh police". Since the message came almost immediately after the question, and even though there is one Radio Traffic audio of 1610 top forty before the message of dad met me, I will delete everything to the right of "dad met me", and save that file as Jane Doe 1A June 6 2008. When the client listens to it, they will hear the question I asked, 1610 top forty and dad met me, and in the spreadsheet where I write in the message received, I will note that 1610 top forty is Radio Traffic.

Next I will open Jane Doe 1 June 6 2008 again, and at the end of the message "dad met me", I will block off and delete everything to the left, and save. I will continue to listen, and if I get a message like "Raleigh Police, Uncle Joe came with him", I will delete Raleigh police, and just save the next message as "Uncle Joe came with him", and save it as Jane Doe 1B June 6 2008. From here I will continue to save only the messages in the form of one or two words, short phrases or complete sentences, preferably minus any radio traffic.

After all the what I call Suspect Paranormal messages have been saved into their own wave files in the order in which they were recorded, the next step in the process is to review the Suspect Paranormal messages saved to try and determine which are Paranormal primarily through validation.

What if however, I have bits and pieces of Radio Traffic in a long message or response to a question? Do I delete the Radio Traffic in that long message? No. In this case, I will leave all the Radio Traffic there. A good example of this scenario is as follows, and is from an actual Show and They Tell recording.

When I held up a carved wooden dolphin, I asked the dead in my room to name the animal, and I heard the following voice messages occur just after I ask my question which was "1610 top forty, fish, Obama said, fish, fish, North Carolina, dolphin, dolphin". For this particular recording, I left it as is, meaning I did not isolate the responses of "fish, fish" or "dolphin, dolphin" into their own wave files. I kept it whole as one unit with the question and answer all in one file.

Suspect Paranormal Voices

If I am engaged in a Show and They Tell recording session, and I am holding up a wrist watch, and I ask the dead in my room to tell me what the name of the item is, and while listening to the recorded file after all Radio Traffic has been identified, I hear the following voice messages "mine is, oh, my, it's watch, over there, it is a watch", the voice messages of "mine is, oh, my, over there" I would deem as Suspect Paranormal. They could be radio traffic I missed identifying, or they could be related to the voice message of watch. They could also be words from other dead in the same recording space having conversations with each other while the one dead answers the question naming the item as a watch, but since I can't discern their meaning, I will classify them as Suspect Paranormal.

When recording a Deceased Loved One recording session, if I ask my dad if he likes the new wine cork tables I made, and I get voice messages that say "pine, my saw, I love them, I made, has a big one, you did a great job", I would deem the voice messages of pine, my saw, I made, has a big one" as Suspect Paranormal mainly because I can't discern how they relate to the wine cork tables I made. Again they could be radio traffic I missed identifying, or they could have resulted from a conversation going on in which only bits and pieces of their conversation were recorded leaving the remainder as missing puzzle pieces.

Some years back when recording for a female client who asked me to contact her mother, her mother made a comment which I identified initially as Suspect Paranormal. A week later, however, the client realized it was indeed Paranormal. I asked her mother if she had seen her grandson, and recorded "Saw Paul got in trouble in school. He said a girl had big boobs". Initially as I mentioned above, this message was identified as Suspect Paranormal because it had no meaning to the client because her son's name is Michael. Later, however, the client got back with me to inform me she remembered her son Michael had gotten in trouble in kindergarten for making comments about a girl's breasts, and after thinking about it she realized and forgot that her son's middle name is Paul. Knowing this, the client accepted this message as Paranormal.

When recording a Known Deceased Missing Person case or even recording a Paranormal Investigation, these voice messages will stay classified as Suspect Paranormal until they can be validated or tied to a person or historical record at which time the voice message would be reclassified as being Paranormal.

Paranormal Voices

Paranormal voice messages per my process are discerned from Suspect Paranormal, and this process is outlined in phase two of chapter ten.

They can be initially identified upon review from a Show and They Tell recording session if the voice message names the item held up, and they can be identified during review of a Deceased Loved One, Known Deceased Missing Person and from a Paranormal Investigation recording session if they can be tied to a person, a thing/s or historical record.

Paranormal Voice messages can also be determined at a later date after the initial review by the client through their own analysis, or if it is a crime case, through found evidence or a confession.

To discern or identify Paranormal voice messages within a Show and They Tell recording session, for example, if I hold up a carved wooden dolphin, and I ask the dead in my room to name the animal, and I hear the following voice messages occur just after I ask my question"1610 top forty, fish, Obama said, fish, fish, North Carolina, dolphin, dolphin", I would deem the voice messages of "fish, fish, fish, dolphin, dolphin" as being Paranormal. They are the answers to my question, and regardless that they occurred within the Radio Traffic, I believe messages of this type are indeed Paranormal.

Likewise if I held up a photograph of a murder victim's husband, and I asked her to tell me what relation this man was to her, and I received the following voice messages of "Husband, Israeli, college, she loved her husband, I love my husband, husband, he was unfaithful", I would deem the voice messages of "Husband, she loved her husband, I love my husband, husband" as being Paranormal because they are answers that relate to her husband. The last message of "he was unfaithful" was initially Suspect Paranormal, but when the case hit the airwaves, police announced to the public that her husband was engaged in an affair.

When trying to determine if a recorded message I transcribe from a Known Deceased Missing Person case recording session is Paranormal, the classification of voice messages is almost always determined by the client unless I have information about the case beforehand from the client which is usually an advocate, or law enforcement. By process, the client would review the printed transcriptions of what I wrote I heard in the recorded files, and try and tie that information to information they already have, or through further investigation try and determine if any of the information received can be used to help them complete their puzzle board and possibly help solve the case. Information recorded that can be tied to existing information they already know, or that can be validated through investigation as being valid, I would classified it as Paranormal. Advocates, private investigators or detectives would basically take what I record, and follow up on it just as they would if they receive a lead through a crime tip line.

A good example involves a missing person case I provided assistance for in recording Radio Sweep (Ghost Box) EVP with the believed dead victim. During the recordings, I kept getting recorded messages of the word "Receipts". I nor the advocate I was working with, and nor the victim's blood relative who worked with the advocate knew what this message meant, initially. The messages got recorded when I was asking the victim if his body was in a pond near his last seen location which we had learned that the pond had never been searched. Based on what was being recorded about Receipts, as well as other recorded information in addition to a Medium's remote view, the advocate arranged a search of that area by one person who when scouting the area surrounding the pond, found a bag of receipts that belonged to the victim. Other potential evidence was found on the banks of the pond, and in the pond additional evidence was found as well.

Due to the evidence found, police were called in and took over the area re-activating what was at this time, a cold case. The recorded word "Receipts" in my opinion was a paranormal message from the deceased victim whose body was later found ten miles away.

Chapter Ten:
Listening to and Transcribing your Files

The next step in the Radio Sweep (Ghost Box) EVP recording process is to listen to, further segment if necessary, de-noise if necessary, and transcribe or write down what Suspect Paranormal or Paranormal voice messages I heard into a Microsoft® Office Excel 2007 worksheet.

In this chapter, I will teach you my two phase transcription process which involves the following:

1. Listening to and saving Suspect Paranormal voice messages into their own wave files. Through client feedback, or if the recording session is of the type Show and They Tell, those that are deemed valid will be reclassified later as Paranormal voice messages

2. Listening to and transcribing all recorded voice messages both Suspect and Paranormal.

The method of listening to and transcription that I use involves using an audio software editing program called Free Audio Editor® http://www.free-audio-editor.com/index.htm in addition to using Microsoft® Excel 2007 worksheets to record any messages.

Phase One:
Isolate and save Suspect and Paranormal Messages

In Phase One of my two step process, I listen to all voice messages that occurred after I asked the question to the deceased. Voice audio messages other than what I have identified as Radio Traffic at this point in the process are classified as Suspect Paranormal until determined otherwise.

Listening to file, Jane Doe 1 June 6 2008, I held up a photograph of a deceased woman's husband, and I asked her what relation was this man was to her, and several voice messages were recorded. In most cases I have found when recording Radio Sweep (Ghost Box) EVP, the answer to my question of the dead does not usually come right after I ask the question as either Radio Traffic or messages that can't be understood will occur before the question is answered.

In this case however, when I asked the deceased woman what relation is this man to you, I recorded an immediate answer of Husband that occurred just after the question was asked with some Radio Traffic recorded thereafter. This particular message that did occur was immediately I classified as being Paranormal because the answer provided was indeed correct and valid.

In the event a Suspect Paranormal or a Paranormal voice message does not occur immediately after I ask the question, I will save the question as one wave file, for example as Jane Doe 1A June 6 2008, and then listen to the original file again until I hear a Suspect Paranormal or Paranormal message, and delete all to the left, and where the message ends in the file, delete all to the right where the message ends, and save that Suspect Paranormal or Paranormal message as Jane Doe 1B June 6 2008.

In wave file Jane Doe 1 June 6 2008, I am now going to edit out the question asked with the first and one of many answers that were recorded thereafter.

The question with the answer is as follows:

"If that lady Jane Doe is with me right now, what relation is that man in the picture on my computer to you? The answer recorded was "Husband."

Using my mouse pointer, I block off all voice messages just after that question with answer of "Husband", and I click the delete key on my computer's keyboard leaving only the question with immediate answer.

Screen Shot (Used with permission of Free Audio Editor)

Now I save the file as Jane Doe 1A June 6 2008, and see below that only the remaining audio will include the question asked with the immediate answer of "Husband".

Screen Shot (Used with permission of Free Audio Editor®)

Next I go back and open the Jane Doe 1 June 6 2008 file, and delete the first question with answer audio and save, so I can proceed to isolate and save the next audio message file following this same process until all Suspect and Paranormal voice messages within each question with answer file have been isolated and saved into their own wave files in the order in which they were recorded.

In the event my client wants to listen to where in the recording session these isolated messages occurred, they can listen to the original wave file I have provided them in the RAW folder.

When I have completed the isolation and saving of the Suspect and or Paranormal voice audio messages, some of which may have Radio Traffic occurring between, delete all original 1, 2, 3, 4, and 5 from the folder of Jane Doe June 6 2008, and use the wave files as noted below to transcribe what you hear on each audio file.

Folder "Jane Doe June 6 2008" should look something like below.

Jane Doe 1A June 6 2008

Jane Doe 1B June 6 2008

Jane Doe 1C June 6 2008

Jane Doe 1D June 6 2008

Jane Doe 1E June 6 2008

Jane Doe 2A June 6 2008

Jane Doe 2B June 6 2008

Jane Doe 2C June 6 2008

Jane Doe 3A June 6 2008

Jane Doe 3B June 6 2008

Jane Doe 3C June 6 2008

Jane Doe 4A June 6 2008

Jane Doe 4B June 6 2008

Jane Doe 5A June 6 2008

Jane Doe 5B June 6 2008

Jane Doe 5C June 6 2008

De-Noise of an Audio Voice Message

De-noising an audio voice message is a process I use on recorded audio voice messages that have or exhibit a lot of static or background noise. If I know there is a message there, one in which I can barely understand, and I want to make it more clear, so my client can hear the message, I will use a De-noise program on that file.

De-noising a Suspect Paranormal or a Paranormal voice audio message is currently being debated as not being an acceptable process by some in the Radio Sweep (Ghost

Box) EVP community as it can degrade the quality of the file every time you run the program.

If you as the reader choose to use a de-noiser program to clear or clean the voice, I recommend you do not clean the file more than once, and use the process sparingly. While there are many different de-noiser programs available on the internet, any one is fine. Just Google® the word de-noiser to clear or clean the voice, and you can pick and choose which one you want.

I personally use an awesome de-noise program called Clear Voice® which can be purchased on the web for about $50.00.

Clear Voice® is a software product from the Speech Technology Center® http://speechpro.com/ . To learn how I use this program to de-noise a file, see Chapter Eight.

Before closing Phase One, I want to stress how very important it is should you record Radio Sweep (Ghost Box) EVP to slice and save every Suspect and Paranormal audio message out into its own wave file after the question has been asked of the dead.

Early on when I first started to record, I would often post only the real time audio messages to web groups I belonged to completely ignoring those other audio voice messages I could not hear real time. Remember previously that I mentioned a real time message is one you can hear during the recording process while you ask the dead questions.

About six months into learning how to listen for messages, I began to notice there were other audio messages there that sounded like a squeaky mouse, hoarse sounding, or whispers, but they just needed to be isolated and saved into their own wave file with increased amplification, so I could hear them more clearly either using head phones or just listening to them outright.

I was shocked to find that I was missing some really important voice audio messages before and after the real time audio messages, and I also found through even further investigation many of the audio messages often occurred in short phrases, complete sentences, or even in small paragraphs. To really understand what I had recorded during my sessions with the dead, I realized that I needed to develop the transcription process writing down all Suspect Paranormal and Paranormal voice audio messages.

Phase Two:
Listen to and Transcribe your Audio Wave Files

Before I show you how I listen to and transcribe my Radio Sweep (Ghost Box) EVP files, I want to make you aware of something really important. Remember as noted previously, it is believed that somehow the dead use words or fragments of speech within the Radio Traffic to form words into audio messages.

Knowing this, you need to understand that just because you record a male or female sounding voice, and this voice is of the human sounding type which has been deemed Paranormal, and if you are recording with a male or female relative, do not expect the recorded audio voice message to sound like your deceased relative when they were alive. When recording with my father, for example, his response messages are recorded as many different voices being male, female sounding, or squeaky mouse, hoarse sounding, and whispers. The sound of his voice he had when alive does not get recorded. I have, however, recorded voices on rare occasions in which some clients through feedback tell me the voice they heard in some of the response messages did sound like their loved one. It can happen, but do not expect it, and do not be discouraged or harbor any suspicions if you hear different voices. To give you a better understand what you may hear in any Radio Sweep (Ghost Box) EVP recording session if you use and follow my process isolating and listening to all messages even those that occur before and after a real time message, I have outlined a fictional response message below.

The message recorded says "Tell the family I miss them", but voice types in each word may be heard as "squeaky mouse = Tell, male = the family, hoarse = I miss, whisper = them". You can also record this above message as all male, all female, all squeaky mouse, all hoarse, or even all whispers.

For some clients I record for trying to get messages from their loved ones, some no matter how hard they try they can't hear all these different voices let alone discern each word in the message mainly because they do not have the day to day experience I have developed over time listening to them. It takes practice listening to them, and the hardest part is the fact each word in each message can and are often a different sounding voice.

My response to these clients is they really should try and learn how to record with their loved ones themselves, and doing so, they will learn how to recognize the different sounding voices, and thereon discern what is being said. Otherwise if they have me continue to record for them, because they do not recognize each voice type or understand what is being said, they will have to take my word what I am hearing in the session. Truly in my opinion it is better to hear and understand these messages yourself, than to take someone else's word for what is being said.

Since you are reading this book, it is obvious to me

you bought it with the intent to learn how to record Radio Sweep (Ghost Box) EVP yourself, and through much practice over time you too will learn the many different voice types and learn also what the dead are telling you or your client, but please keep this in mind in that any client you record for, they may not understand a word of the recorded messages, and this is due in part to their recognizing the different voice types and understand what those voices are saying.

After each question with answer file has been reviewed isolating each Suspect or Paranormal message into their own wave file, it is time to listen to and transcribe each message into some format you and or your client can easily read.

Before I begin to discuss the following process, I want to make you aware how I try to accurately write down what I heard. I listen to the response messages from the questions I asked, and I write what I heard phonetically how they sound not being really concerned about correct spelling.

If you were to engage this process, you will see most of what you write down, if not all will have correct spelling, however some messages will make no sense at all. Still it is important to write them down anyway.

The reason it is important to write down every suspect or paranormal message phonetically how they sound, especially if you are recording for a client, is the very sound of that message even if misspelled, the client through reading and listening to it, may know exactly what that message is. If you neglect to consider it a valid message not transcribing it, you have thrown away a message the dead have for their loved one, one their loved one understands, even though you believe it has no meaning because perhaps you can't spell it.

One crime victim I recorded with kept saying something over and over in different recording sessions, and I could not spell it out for transcription, so by listening to it and writing down what I heard phonetically, I came up with an acronym of CRX. This message even though it could not be spelled out matching any dictionary as a valid word, proved to be a valid message only his aunt knew. Her nephew had a souped-up hot rod car, and he teased his aunt about her little four cylinder Honda® CRX.

Another example in which writing down all messages that can't be spelled is important, involves recording by a living cancer researcher with a deceased cancer researcher for information how to cure cancer. When listening to and transcribing response messages, the word that you the recorder writes down phonetically, one you can't spell, may be a valid medical term, and through discussion with other researchers, the very sound of that message may be identified. Likewise if you are recording for answers to questions a medical researcher gave you to ask, and if you write down everything phonetically into your worksheet, what you thought was not a real word, the medical researcher reading it or even listening to it may recognize it as valid.

Transcription Process

I prefer to transcribe or write down what I hear in my audio files into a Microsoft® Office Excel 2007 worksheet with each file listed in the order in which it was recorded. The worksheet will be my puzzle board in which I will assemble all recorded audio messages to try and understand what the dead are telling me or what they are telling my client.

Screen Shot (Used with permission of Microsoft®)

For me since I primarily record for clients, I always set up my client files in a main folder on my computer with a sub folder that represents the date that the recording took place, and within the sub folder are the segmented audio files I will listen to and transcribe. Also located within the sub folder is the Microsoft® Office Excel 2007 worksheet file which I will use for all Radio Sweep (Ghost Box) EVP recordings I engage for this client.

The sub file name in column D is the isolated audio message file I will listen to, and in column E is where I add the question I asked of the deceased spirit. Any answers or messages I transcribe from the dead are added to column F leaving column G for the classification of Suspect or Paranormal, and column H is used for the voice types of the squeaky mouse, hoarse, whisper, and human sounding.

While listening to these files it is common that you may have to segment some of these files again to ensure the message can be heard more clearly by you or the client. The reason for further segmentation revolves around the fact that some voice messages tend to be compressed. Think of it this way, if you take a large wide rubber band and stretch it out, and you write a sentence, and then release the rubber band, you may be able to make out a few words. By segmenting these audio files into even smaller units, the compressed messages which often sound garbled become clearer when they are sliced out like a stick of butter into their own wave file. For example, let's say that file Jane Doe 1B June 6 2008 is not really clear, so I slice it in half, and save it as two separate files, so the client can hear the message more clearly. This file will now be saved as follows:

- Jane Doe 1B1 June 6 2008

- Jane Doe 1B2 June 6 2008

If for any reason I need to slice up Jane Doe 1B2 June 6 2008 again, the file now changes to Jane Doe 1B2a June 6 2008 and Jane Doe 1B2b June 6 2008.

What is very important is each time you slice, you save it in the order in which it was recorded as the client may want to go back to listen to the original file Jane Doe June 6 2008 located in the folder named RAW to listen to where in that file this message occurred. While I have never had a client do this, you should always keep that option open.

For file Jane Doe 1A June 6 2008, when I listened to this file, the audio message I heard was "Husband". Since this response occurred after I asked "If that lady Jane Doe is with me right now, what relation is that man in the picture on my computer to you?", I re-classified it from Suspect to Paranormal because it relates to the photograph of the deceased woman's husband I had displayed on my computer screen. This particular message for your information was of the hoarse sounding type.

Screen Shot (Used with permission of Microsoft®)

For the next message from file Jane Doe 1B June 6 2008, I heard another message of "I need to tell you" which was a squeaky mouse sounding voice. I left this audio message classified as Suspect Paranormal because I am not really sure how it relates to the photograph.

Screen Shot (Used with permission of Microsoft®)

Listening even further, and you should now see and understand the process, I have identified two more Paranormal audio messages, and one Suspect Paranormal.

Screen Shot (Used with permission of Microsoft®)

Question	Answers	Classification	Voice Type
If that lady Jane Doe is with me right now, what relation is that man in the picture on my computer to you?	Husband	Paranormal - relates to photograph	Hoarse sounding
	I need to tell you	Suspect Paranormal	Squeaky mouse sounding
	And he's "?"	Suspect Paranormal	Whisper sounding
	She loved her husband	Paranormal - relates to photograph	Human sounding
	I love my husband and I miss him	Paranormal - relates to photograph	Hoarse sounding

As you listen to your files using Free Audio

Editor® or any other audio editing software, these programs have many different features in which you can raise or lower the volume, speed up or slow down the message, further clean or even reverse a message to see if it has meaning in a reversed position. While I do reverse some messages that I can't understand at all, I do not give those to the client, as reversing them changes them from how they were originally recorded.

As mentioned previously, listening to and transcribing these Radio Sweep (Ghost Box) EVP audio files I must tell you is not easy for the beginner let alone a client, but over time, and especially if you spend a great deal of time recording the Show and They Tell type of recordings, you will quickly learn to hear and understand audio voice messages of the type squeaky mouse sounding, hoarse sounding, whispers, and even learn how to differentiate what human sounding voices are potential Radio Traffic verses Suspect or Paranormal voices.

What is really important, and I can't stress this enough, is you need to slice the files up, and segment them into smaller units to help ensure you isolate every Suspect or Paranormal message in that file, and write them down phonetically as you hear them. Early on when I first started recording, I missed so many messages that were occurring before and after the real time messages.

In closing this chapter, remember to use your mouse pointer to block off and listen to the entire file in small increments from left to right, and if need be, slice off or segment more Suspect or Paranormal messages into their own wave files, so they can be heard more clearly. While the process I have outlined above may seem to some as a lot of work, the results you will find will in most cases will be astounding! Recording and posting a real time message, one that can be heard during the recording session, is indeed a treat, but to capture and isolate all those other messages that occur before and after a real time message, these are the messages that when transcribed in the order in which they were recorded, that often assemble into paragraph form.

Chapter Eleven:
Preparing Files for Yourself or a Client

After I have completed a Radio Sweep (Ghost Box) EVP recording session, I follow the below process for each type of recording.

If my recording was a "Show and They Tell" session, I would print a copy of the transcribed worksheet, and make a CD of the recorded files making sure the Microsoft® Office Excel 2007 worksheet is also included on that CD. Next, I will place the printed transcription and CD into a manila folder in my filing cabinet with the date the "Show and They Tell" recording session took place.

If my recording was of the type "Deceased Loved One" with any of my deceased family members, I would do the same as above, but if this recording was for a Client, I would do one of two things depending on how the client wants to get access to listen to and review the material. I may create a secure web page where I would upload the files and transcriptions, a web page in which the client can control who has access to view and listen to the material, or I may mail a CD and printed transcription along with a cover letter to the client.

In that cover letter I briefly explain how I record and transcribe Radio Sweep (Ghost Box) EVP; I explain how it is believed the dead use words within the Radio Traffic to form words, phrases and sentences as messages, and I also explain since there is the possibility that other deceased could be present and talk during the time I have recorded with their loved one. I also advise the client should listen to what has meaning to them and disregard the rest until they can be validated.

I would like to remind each of you that may engage a "Deceased Loved One" recording session for a client to ask the client before initiating that recording session if they want to receive and listen to any negative messages. I have found even if I record let's say five nice and loving messages, but two additional are negative in which let's say the deceased is unhappy with one or more of the living relatives, the client will tend to remember the negative messages, and the whole experience of their wanting you to make contact with their loved one to hear how they are will turn out to be a negative experience. Always remember that any negative message can be from the client's loved one, but it can also be from a Dark Head, a negative spirit trying to hose up the recording session giving you wrong information. During one of my client recording sessions, I actually heard a voice that said "Stop saying that! This is my recording session!"

When recording Radio Sweep (Ghost Box) EVP for a "Paranormal Investigation", remember to always contact the group leader to ask permission to use the device, and if allowed, ask how they want you to compile and present any findings.

If my recording session was a "Known Deceased Missing Person" session, I follow the same process as I would for a "Known Deceased Loved One" recording, but explain in the cover letter since other deceased spirits can chime in during the recording session, and since I do not know for sure if all messages recorded are indeed from the victim, I advise all recorded messages be followed up on as any lead would through a crime tip line, and as noted previously please if at all possible only give this information to an advocate, a private investigator that would relay any info to police, or to only give this information to a law enforcement professional. If a Dark Head has taken over all or part of your recording session giving you sickly and disturbing detail how the victim died, and if you give that wrong information to a family member, you can do serious harm to that person. Leave it up to the professionals to decide what to do with any information you receive through a recording session with a victim.

Chapter Twelve:
Radio Sweep (Ghost Box) EVP Cases

As the reader of this book about Radio Sweep (Ghost Box) Electronic Voice Phenomena, you have learned what the meaning of Radio Sweep electronic voice phenomena is. You have read and learned about the history of Radio Sweep (Ghost Box) EVP; you have learned about speaking to the dead with radios, you have learned what real time spirit communication is, you have learned what the best radios are to purchase and hack, and you have learned about Dark Heads , Demons and Technicians. You have also learned what the preferred equipment is, how to make an appointment with the dead, you have learned about the construct of the recording session itself, how to upload and convert your files, how to segment and de-noise your files, how to classify your recorded paranormal suspect and paranormal messages, you have learned how to listen to and transcribe your suspect and paranormal recorded messages, and you have learned how to prepare your recorded files for a client.

Knowing the above, if you were to procure and hack the right equipment today, and thereon follow this process step by step, what would you learn from an actual Radio Sweep (Ghost Box) EVP recording session.

As previously mentioned, when I first started recording and listening to Radio Sweep (Ghost Box) EVP recording sessions, I would only listen to the high sounding messages, which when classified as paranormal, they equate as real time spirit communication, RTSC, a term coined by Steve Hultay of Keyport Paranormal®. However, when I began to engage in more recording sessions, and I toyed with audio editors and de-noisers, I quickly learned there were more messages that occurred before and after these real time spirit communication messages.

To help you better understand what you can expect to learn from each of your recording sessions whether they are engaged with a "Known Deceased Loved One, a Known Deceased Missing Person, or from a Paranormal Investigation", I have outlined below some of my key and most interesting cases.

Please note that in most cases, I have changed the names of all persons involved to help ensure their identities are not divulged and are kept secret.

Known Deceased Loved One Cases

The Fire Chief and Grandmother

The following case involves my recording simultaneously with my friend's deceased father, a retired New York fire chief, and his one hundred two year old grandmother both who passed very close to each other in time. Most of the messages recorded were classified as

Paranormal by the client leaving the remainder as Suspect Paranormal.

David Alamance Junior's father, David Alamance Senior, passed after a long battle with cancer. David Junior took care of his father throughout his entire ordeal providing in home health care, taking his father to and from the hospital or doctor's offices, in addition to working a full time job.

In addition to caring for his ailing father, David Junior also cared for his aging mother and his one hundred two year old grandmother mind you who lived alone in her own home a short distance away. David Junior was a son greatly admired who literally gave his entire life to care for his parents and grandmother. David truly is a living Angel who to this day now cares for his mother.

Not long after David Alamance Junior's father and grandmother passed, David and I had a discussion about my using a recorder and a hacked radio to speak with the dead. I offered to try and make contact with his father and grandmother to which he replied an emphatic yes!

He asked me to get messages from his father, and specifically asked me to ask his grandmother what her favorite sport was. David Junior's grandmother was one hundred two years old when she died, and she played this sport up until she passed.

On November 10, 2008 I engaged a Radio Sweep (Ghost Box) EVP recording session with David Alamance Junior's father and grandmother which started off like this "Radio is on and scanning", messages received were "And I miss hugging you, yes we miss you"

Next I asked "If David Alamance Junior's father is

here today, what is David's brother's first name?" This particular question if answered correctly would indicate to me, the spirit in attendance is Mr. David Alamance Senior, however, the question was not answered, and I received a message that said "Know this from me. I love you"

Next I asked the confirmation question of David Junior's grandmother, "If David Alamance Junior's grandmother is here today, what is your favorite sport? What did you like to play?" I received a response of "I loved to go golfing". David Alamance Junior confirmed this message as an accurate confirmation this was his grandmother as she did play golf even at one hundred two years old.

Next I asked Mr. Alamance Senior if he had any messages for his son, and received the following messages that are each saved in the order in which they were recorded in as their own wave file.

- I miss you
- David helped me to go and visit "?", don't forget (Note "?" indicates a message I did not discern even phonetically)
- First I go to, and you're not even home
- David l love you
- David helped me to get through all this

Next I asked "Mr. Alamance Senior do you have a special message to say to your lovely wife Marissa. Would you like to say something to her right now?" Messages received were "I see your family. Tory is good. Miss you, and we miss you"

While listening to and transcribing this recording session, I was amazed at what had been recorded. Here is a man who truly loved his son, and truly appreciated all his son did for him taking care of his father up until his last second of life.

Next I asked Mr. Alamance Senior who he met when he crossed over, and received the following messages each saved in their own wave file.

- My uncle saw me
- Andersen met me. I saw him
- One of us saw Nixon, the president!

Now imagine that seeing a former president of the United States, I bet that was an amazing experience, one that would likely not have happened in real life.

After I completed asking David Alamance Junior's father questions, I started to ask the grandmother if she had any messages for her daughter and received the following messages. "Cause your family took care of me. Ask you David, tell your mom you got hold of me. She likes her David. David cause you're patient with me. Of course he did, he loved you. He was always waiting for daddy. He loves how much you did. "

After listening to the above messages, I got the impression while the grandmother was relaying her messages, she was also having a conversation with someone else in the spirit world about what her grandson David had done. I noticed this in the message "Of course he did, he loved you".

Next I asked the grandmother again what her favorite sport was that she liked to play, and received the following two messages.

- I guess you're talking to me
- Go golfing. I golf in the morning

Truly this was an amazing Radio Sweep (Ghost Box) EVP recording session, however, I want to make sure you understand that not all recording sessions with a Known Deceased Loved One will turn out this nice. In my experience thus far, whether it is recording with my own deceased family members, or recording with a client's family members, there have been sessions in which the dead have messaged back negative remarks about what they do not like the living relatives are doing or how they are acting. For example, during one client recording with a client's deceased mother, the mother made negative remarks about her living husband's girlfriend.

The Lifeguard

Lifeguards are expert swimmers that watch over to help protect or even rescue swimmers in trouble. Like policeman or firemen, lifeguards often risk their own lives helping others.

Like Mr. Alamance Senior mentioned previously, Thomas Banicheck, a well respected father, husband and lifeguard of Long Island, New York, lost his battle with cancer. Thomas's cancer was of the worst kind in which it had traveled throughout his entire body leaving him with no option for recovery. His mother in law Melody Anderson, as well as Thomas's wife and children were praying for the best right down to the final hours.

Melody Anderson, my workmate, was an amazing woman. She amazingly came to work every day, I think perhaps to keep her mind busy. Daily and weekly, she shared Thomas's condition and status.

One April afternoon Melody contacted me to inform me that Thomas had passed away. Melody knew through prior discussions that I spoke to the dead using radio sweep devices, and she asked me if after the funeral I could try and get in touch with Thomas to get messages back to her daughter Vanessa. Without hesitation, I told her yes, and moved one of my other client appointments out due to this emergency.

On April 29th, 2009 I engaged a Radio Sweep (Ghost Box) EVP recording with Thomas Banicheck. Immediately just after I had turned on the recorder and the hacked radio to scan mode, even before I could ask a question, I received the following message "Death is early. He is alright". Next I asked "Good Morning. Is there a Thomas Banicheck of Long Island, New York here today", and I received the following messages which are saved in their own wave file in the order in which they were recorded.

- Tell my family you hear of "?"
- I'm ok
- I'm amazed you do it for
- It will be a serving to me
- This last Sunday morning
- Enjoy her. I love you for missing me
- Jim come to see me. And then we catch a wave
- Listen he is sitting on an
- He told me about the family
- You'll get my t-shirt

Now, before I proceed to the next question, perhaps you are wondering why I did not leave all these messages in one wave file. Had I done that, they would have been compressed, and you would not have heard them all. File segmentation is very important as noted in Chapter Eight. Some words in the messages are lower sounding, and if you do not segment and split up the files into smaller units, you will only hear the higher volume words and miss the complete message the dead are sending to you.

Next I asked "Thomas Banicheck, if you are here, can you please tell me what your wife's first name is?" Messages received were as follows.

- I'm a long ways to listen to Thomas singing to my dad
- I have the best family!
- He calls for Vanessa. He is pissed his phone is not here
- Tell them I said
- God say to me. You heard me
- It's a good morning to see you
- Fun for the action. That you hear from me. That I didn't know
- In the left lane, I need to know how he did it

Note above that Thomas said his wife's name "Vanessa".

What happened with the next question with answers is truly amazing. Remember that I told you that Thomas Banicheck is a lifeguard, and a lifeguard saves lives. Even in death, Thomas Banicheck is helping save lives.

After I asked "Thomas Banicheck, if you are here, can you see and hear your wife and family in their home", I received the following messages.

- **Of course Vanessa will listen. You'll see**
- They want to see me often
- Frank's not hearing me, but she could be pregnant
- **Oh! And your electric burner! Check the window**
- His clothes are laying on my bed
- His mommy does say this. That's her job
- I'm totally pissed or amazed. Lost your life and he can hear me
- Totally amazed you heard about me

Two key messages above are highlighted in red, and for

good reason. Shortly after I mailed the recording and printed transcriptions over to Melody I received the following e-mail from her.

"Vanessa appreciated the info from you. One thing that didn't make any sense ended up in a day or so to make sense. Vanessa is re-doing their family room. Here is what she wrote to me (I told you about the plumbing issue with my furnace and radiator. There was a part mentioned that said you'll see. Vanessa will listen, and then something was said about the electric burner under the window. The radiator under the window was leaking into the rotted out floor. When they turned the heat off to fix the radiator, they discovered the valve on the heater was broken, and would have started to leak carbon monoxide into the house when I turned it on this winter. So I went back to the transcript, and I think Thomas was trying to say something about that."

Once a lifeguard, always a lifeguard, even in spirit!

Jesus Christ

Recently in conversation with some of my paranormal peers, we began to talk about our Radio Sweep (Ghost Box) EVP recordings we each had engaged in, and the topic came up whether any of us had ever recorded or had tried to record with Jesus Christ. My response was swift and precise that I had recorded with Jesus Christ as did I also record with Jesus mother, the Blessed Virgin Mary. I actually have two Yahoo® web groups set up in which I have posted some of my recordings with Jesus as well as with his mother. They are as follows.

- http://groups.yahoo.com/group/EVP-ITC-With-Jesus-Christ/?yguid=338683728
- http://groups.yahoo.com/group/EVP-ITC-MessagesWithMaryTheBlessedVirgin/?yguid=3386837 28

Being raised Catholic I was taught to pray to Jesus, the Blessed Virgin Mary, to God and to the Holy Spirit for help and guidance, so I had no fear or issue in trying to make contact directly with Jesus Christ using radio sweep technology.

On May 25th, 2010 I engaged my first Radio Sweep (Ghost Box) EVP recording with Jesus Christ, and just after asking "Good morning is Jesus Christ here today?" I recorded the following message "You have good passion, and I have been watching you". I immediately classified this message as Paranormal as intuitively I felt it was indeed Jesus speaking to me.

The next message simultaneously occurred while I asked Jesus if he had a message for the world. To listen to it one must block out what I am saying to hear the message, and just after this message another series of messages occurred in response to the same question. Each message is saved in its own mp3 file.

The messages are as follows.

- **In this box, I want to speak to you about your country**
- **I said the chief, he killed all nature**
- His box he hopes will bring them back to live with him and Mary
- I would like to see if you could live in peace with me

After hearing the first two messages, I initially wanted to classify them as Paranormal, but classified them as Suspect Paranormal. I got the impression Jesus was referring to the Gulf oil spill which occurred in April a month before this recording session had taken place. As for the third response, I got the impression Jesus was referring to my Radio Sweep (Ghost Box) EVP device as being perhaps a catalyst that would bring people around the world closer to him and Mary, the Blessed Virgin, and the last message I believe coincides with the third message in that Jesus wants to see the world at peace.

After this initial recording with Jesus Christ, I was so excited about the results, that I asked my Guardian Angel to set up additional recording sessions with Jesus Christ on the following dates.

- June 1, 2010
- June 11, 2010
- June 17, 2010

For the June 1 2010 Radio Sweep (Ghost Box) EVP recording session with Jesus Christ, just after I asked Jesus how we can fix the oil leak, I recorded "My Lord they have come here to try and meet you", and for this particular message I emphatically classified it as a Paranormal message.

Next I asked Jesus to help me get a better radio, and recorded the following messages each saved into their own mp3 file.

- He prayed for you to go to me
- Not that I need you. It's called almighty
- I'd be interested in doing this, nice talking to you today.

The radio I have even to this day which is the hacked Radio Shack® model 12-469 radio, one no longer in production, has an annoying clicking sound on the AM band, and unfortunately the AM band is where the best messages are recorded. Through intuition, I classified these messages as Paranormal.

Now the next response from the question "Jesus is there anything that you want the world to know that is very important", recorded as " "?" **Missile Strike next Saturday!"** which drove me bonkers as I did not know what to do. Here I am recording with Jesus Christ, and I get a message about an up and up and coming missile strike and anyone in their right mind would think I was crazy if I had alerted the authorities, so I alerted a few close friends, and watched the news saying prayers the strike would not occur.

Since the recording session occurred on June 1, 2010, my first thought is the missile strike would occur on the coming Saturday June 5th, however a good friend of mine told me she felt the message meant the next Saturday after the coming Saturday, and if that was indeed what Jesus was referring to, then perhaps he knew that on June 12th, 2010 Israel had secured permission from Saudi Arabia to fly through their air space for a test run to bomb Iran's nuclear facilities.
http://forum.prisonplanet.com/index.php?topic=174686.0

I actually recorded with Jesus Christ at eight AM on June 12th, but at the time did not know of the planned test bombing run until later when my friend contacted me to tell me.

Is it possible that maybe Israel actually had planned to bomb Iran then on that day, but the plan was averted somehow? When I recorded with Jesus Christ on June 12th, when I asked him about the missile strike, his messages alluded to a horrible disaster that would affect multitudes of people.

Lastly when I said thanks to Jesus for coming to the June 1 2010 recording session, I received the following two responses each saved into their own mp3 file in the order in which they were recorded.

- Michael I pray for you
- Mary want to get with you. She's waiting for you. The message that we know you will listen to me

As noted above, on June 12 2010 I engaged another Radio Sweep (Ghost Box) EVP recording session with Jesus Christ to try and find out what day the missile strike would occur as it had not occurred on June 5th. Seconds after I turned the radio sweep device on to scan mode, I received an instant message that said "Christ Jesus! Michael we love you. "?"" and where I have the question mark means there are words there I could not understand.

Next I asked Jesus about when the missile strike would occur, and received the following two messages saved in their own mp3 file just after I asked the question.

- Tell the president. They plan this response a recipe through Satan
- They have called please kill it and they heard

The above messages were recorded at eight AM EST in Cary, North Carolina on June 12th 2010, the same day Saudi Arabia had given Israel permission to fly through their air space to do a test bombing run against Iran's nuclear facilities. Again as noted previously is it possible that somehow a real bombing run was averted? Only Israel and the US government would know the answer to that question.

On June 17th 2010 I engaged another Radio Sweep (Ghost Box) EVP recording session with Jesus Christ to ask him if we were experiencing the End of Days and received the following messages.

- There is a lot going to happen, and he says that you can help me
- Ask him he need to tell you
- And there will be explosions, and the people "?"
- A lot of people will pray for your family

From an analysis perspective in review of the last two messages of June 12, 2010 and the above messages from the June 17 2010 recording session, are they Paranormal or Suspect Paranormal? Those received from the June 12th recording session I would deem as Suspect Paranormal because I have no information that supports the responses as being true, and even still I have no information that supports the responses as being true, but they are in my opinion answers to my question. For these I am caught between classifying them as Paranormal or Suspect Paranormal.

In addition to my review, especially since the responses indicate impending doom coming our way, and due to the fact that I did make an appointment to record with Jesus Christ on these two days, one might believe that since I captured a recorded message from who I believe is Jesus Christ that the messages are indeed true.

My best advice to anyone that records Radio Sweep (Ghost Box) EVP or to anyone that uses a recorder only to capture EVP – Electronic Voice Phenomena, if any messages received are about impending doom coming your way, pray it does not happen, but do not believe it as a matter of fact. There are spiritual beings that can and often do give out false information, beings you have no clue who they are, who can take advantage of let's say a no show by Jesus Christ and give you false information. It happens, and I have experienced receiving wrong information during some of my cases.

The Blessed Virgin Mary

After great success in recording Radio Sweep (Ghost Box) EVP with Jesus Christ, I made it a point to try and make contact and record with Jesus mother, the Blessed Virgin Mary. Like Jesus, I wanted to hear what the Virgin Mary wanted me and the world to know.

Throughout history the Blessed Virgin Mary more often than any other religious icon has made herself known and visible to key people throughout the world, more so than her son Jesus. While I am no one special, I was truly amazed that I too could reach her, and so can you!

On June 29, 2010 I engaged my first and presently my only recording to date with the Blessed Virgin Mary asking her several questions. After I asked the Blessed Virgin Mary if she had a message for the world, I recorded the following messages each saved into their own wave file in the order in which they were recorded.

- What can we say to the people
- May God love Mary. Listen Now you receive the Blessed Mother
- Everybody believe in your cause, and Mary?? loves you
- We "?" Jesus love you

The next question I asked the Blessed Virgin Mary only resulted with one response. I asked if she had a message for religious world leaders, and received a response of "I said when I met your family. That real soon you'll be helping me"

After I asked the Blessed Virgin Mary if she had a message for me, I received the following messages each recorded and saved in the order in which they were recorded in.

- Ask you. Go see my son. Be careful. I can hear
- My children they're wanting to meet you
- Listen I have seen me through you
- Your family is watching when you get close, and they'll come and get you

After hearing and transcribing the above messages, I literally had tears in my eyes. These messages were very different from the Virgin Mary, so very different than from Jesus Christ her son. When listening to the messages from Jesus Christ, it was almost as if I was receiving messages from a sibling or male friend, whereas the messages from the Virgin Mary were mother like messages, being very gentle and loving.

At the end of the recording session, I said goodbye to the Virgin Mary and thanked her for coming, and received this last and final message which said "?" This works. Well done. Now you know that her is the teacher of you"

This was indeed an amazing recording with the Virgin Mary as was the recording with her son Jesus Christ! What is even more amazing is they each took the time to record with me, and it is my firm belief they will take the time to record with anyone who makes an attempt to reach them whether it is through using my Radio Sweep (Ghost Box) EVP process or just using s simple tape or digital recorder.

What is important for each of you reading this book to know is that you too can set up appointments to meet with your religious leaders, your family and friends to ask for help and guidance. Anyone with an open mind can do this, and while it does take practice to hear and understand the higher and lower sounding words at the same time, even to understand raspy, electronic and in-human sounding voices, once you learn the process, it will be like learning to ride a bike for the first time. It is an experience you will never forget.

Known Deceased Missing Person Case

Since I first began recording Known Deceased Missing Person cases as well as Crime cases starting April 12th, 2008 to date, I have recorded twenty five cases, most of which are still under investigation.

Within this section, I will discuss a drowning victim whose body had yet to be found, but was eventually found, and I will also be discussing some key missing person crime cases I recorded which by lack of the right experience many setbacks and issues surfaced as a result. It is the missing person crime cases that I really want to make you aware of what can go wrong if you the initiator of this type of recording session do not have the right experience or background. Please note that all names of all people involved in these cases have been changed to protect their identity.

The Drowning Victim

On September 23rd, 2008 shortly after I had created a new Yahoo® paranormal discussion group named EVP-ITC-SDWR-SpeakingToTheDeadWithRadios-, through this group I met and started to engage private discussions with a new member about a family member of hers that had been swept underwater near a canal lock in Ohio. Betty Johnson who soon became my client asked me to try and make contact with her family member whose body had yet to be found.

- For this particular recording session, I asked and received responses for over forty questions, and since I was given information about the presumed deceased client and the circumstances surrounding her disappearance, I was able to classify some of the recorded messages as being Paranormal. All other messages were classified as Suspect Paranormal to which could be re-classified if the client determined they had meaning. For purposes of this chapter, and the lesson you will learn from reading it, I will only discuss a handful of those questions I asked with responses.

Four days before the planned recording session, Betty Johnson provided me a list of questions to ask her presumed deceased loved one whom I shall call Angel Johnson. Betty wanted to know where Angel's body was, and she also wanted to know whom Angel wanted to raise her son Gabriel. The family was expected to attend a court hearing to try and make that determination, and they needed to know the answer to this question if at all possible. The following are the list questions Betty Johnson wanted me to ask Angel. In addition to these questions, I also asked additional questions.

- Will we recover her body?
- If her body will be recovered, when will we find her?
- Please tell us who she wants to raise her son Gabriel. Does she want Jenny, Mary, Belinda, or Tracy to raise her son?

With this information at hand, I immediately began to pray to my Guardian Angel to ask my guide to find Angel Johnson in the spirit world, and to have her meet me on September 27th at eight am for a recording session. I asked my guide to please explain to Angel who I was, that I wanted to make contact with her to try and get messages back to her family.

On the day of the recording, and before I turned the recorder and my hacked Radio Shack® 12-469 radio on, I explained to Angel who I was, that I could not see her nor could I hear her, but that I could hear any messages she may have that get picked up on the digital recorder I had laying besides the external speaker that was plugged into the hacked radio. I also explained to Angel the process I was about to engage, and explained to her when I was asking a question, I needed her to not say anything to me, and to wait until I stopped asking the question. The reason I ask the dead to wait before speaking is because if they do speak, their messages can be heard while I am talking. Next I explained to Angel when she heard me say the word OK, that was a signal to her to stop talking, and that I was going to ask another question.

After the preliminary explanation of my process and after my introduction was completed, I said the following prayer. "Almighty God and Jesus, please bless this recording session, and please help ensure I only record messages that are from Angel Johnson. I ask if there are other spirits in my room watching to please not speak or say anything because if you do, the recorder will also record your messages too which makes it difficult for the family that will listen to this recording to determine if the messages are from their loved one."

After the prayer, I turned the recorder on, and I turned the radio on to scan forward mode, and starting asking questions.

The first question I asked was "Good Spirits is there an Angel Johnson here today from Milan, Ohio?" Recorded messages revealed "Yes, asking her to listen to you, was pretty, people here with me, this us, must have been fifteen that day."

All of the above messages I classified as Paranormal with exception to "must have been fifteen that

135

day" which I classified as Suspect Paranormal. Ultimately the client will be the one who will through reading and listening to the recorded messages will determine if this message has meaning, and if it does, then I would classify it as Paranormal.

From my perspective, the response "Yes", and the next response of "asking her to listen to you" I believe relates to my asking the question if she was here today. The responses of "was pretty, people here with me" I believe are messages she was a pretty girl and that there are other spirits in my home with her during the recording session.

Next instead of asking a question, I just said "Angel your Aunt Betty asked me to get in touch with you". Recorded messages revealed "She's a dead mom. Ask her a question, beginning of me be the one, me pleased her, your more familiar with what's best for me, we love the show us pain, the only ones we know, high school friends look for me."

Through analysis of these recorded messages, "She's a dead mom" I believe is Paranormal as it relates to the drowning. "Ask her a question, beginning of me be the one, me pleased her, your more familiar with what's best for me, we love the show us pain, the only ones we know, high school friends look for me" I classified as Suspect Paranormal. The client may understand these messages, and if they do, then whichever the client understands would be re-classified as Paranormal.

When I asked this question "The family wants to know the first and last name of the person that you want to raise and take care of your son?", the first response I received was "Great people Jenny's family, and they only." Now this particular response was amazing because Jenny is one of the people her aunt provided as a possible person to raise her son Gabriel. Since it relates to names provided as possible persons to raise her son, I classified this message as Paranormal.

In addition to the above response saved as its own wav file, there was also another response that I believe relates to her situation in the water. These messages said "It hurts. Legs against the wall. I'm here to the right of the fence. Milly's planning to show off. The police go home. Don't see ya? Good bye for me. If they look they will find I am here. Tore up fish nets I'm knee deep near the last pump or home?" All of these in my opinion are Paranormal and relate to the drowning with exception to "Milly's planning to show off". That message about Milly is a mystery, but it could have meaning to the family or friends.

Now after reading the above messages, I can only imagine what you the reader must be thinking. Where in the world did Angel drown, you might have thought? Angel Johnson while fishing waded too far near a canal lock or dam, and she got sucked under and got stuck in between the first and the second wall of the dam never going over. From what I have learned about these type dams or locks is that opening between the first and the second and final wall, the final wall being the one where the water spills over, that opening is called a vortex. If anything falls in it, it stays in the vortex circling around and around near the bottom until it is eventually kicked out.

Therefore, knowing the above workings of the lock or dam, and after listening to and transcribing those messages, I believe they relate to the dam and perhaps the insides of the vortex itself. Only Angel knows for sure, but my impression by these messages is she was describing her ordeal.

For the next question, I asked Angel "And Angel

can you tell me where your body is located", and recorded messages received were "Back Bedroom, in my sneakers. Pink slip from burnell for shop, lift, book. She lost it. It was missing. Jetties, Doug, we fish. But kissed. It was in the papers. I went in. Long knickers? Express. For a while I was safe, missed chest? Call missed. "I am at a telephone calling you". Baby. We have looked. Instrument. And we fish, the most dangerous."

Messages of "Back Bedroom, in my sneakers. Pink slip from burnell for shop, lift, book. She lost it. It was missing. Doug, but kissed. It was in the papers. Long knickers? Express, missed chest, call missed. "I am at a telephone calling you". Baby. We have looked. Instrument." I classified as Suspect Paranormal, however, the client did find a receipt inside the sneakers, so that message was re-classified as Paranormal.

Messages of "Jetties, we fish. I went in. For a while I was safe, missed chest? And we fish, the most dangerous." I classified as Paranormal as they relate in my opinion to her fishing and the canal lock.

This next question with answers to me reveals how Angel drowned as described by the client. I asked "Angel is there any way that you can come over here and stand next to me" At this moment while asking the question, I forgot what I was going to say, and messages that followed said "She's in. My sisters watch me, must swim. Them feet swept down. Who was with us. They fish. I go to john. People watch me go under"

Based on the above, and the fact that the client said Angel was wading and got sucked under, most of the above messages from Angel describe her demise to a tee.

Remembering what I was going to ask Angel, I

proceeded to ask the remaining part of the above question, "Angel can you see my computer" During thus particular question session, I had displayed on my computer a photograph of the canal and lock where she went under the water. Messages received were "Watch me, people do, fishing. I grab my toes" These messages I classified as Paranormal because they describe the scene as described to me by the client. Angel was wade fishing near the canal lock, and there were other people there at the time of the accident. Angel's body was finally recovered September 27th, 2008

Angel's responses to the forty plus questions I asked her revealed the person she wanted to raise her son, described the area surrounding the canal lock/dam, and described just how she met her fate. And while not discussed here, Angel also provided a myriad of personal messages back to her family and provided descriptions of where she is now, a place we all know as Heaven!

The Missing Teen

Earlier I mentioned that I started recording Known Deceased Missing Person cases beginning April 12th, 2008, but what I did not tell you was that I first started recording Radio Sweep (Ghost Box) EVP early February 2008. Imagine for a moment any person with very little experience using these recording devices attempting to record with a presumed deceased crime victim. Imagine also this same person had no prior experience in the paranormal whatsoever prior to that time. This person was me.

The missing teen case I am about to discuss with you was my first crime case I recorded Radio Sweep (Ghost Box) EVP for, and my getting involved came about in an unexpected way. Remember I started recording

February 2008, but by April 2008 after recording and receiving some truly amazing messages from the dead, voices that called out my first and my last name, I had become bored with recording and just uploading these files for my new found friends to hear. It was when I confided in a friend, Juli Velasquez, whom I met in Frank Sumption's "EVP-ITC · EVP and ITC discussion Group" on Yahoo® that I learned these devices could be used to help solve crime and missing person cases.

Juli explained she was a Medium as well was also a former Chicago police officer, and that she used her mediumistic skills as well as radio sweep devices to get information from the dead to try and solve cases. She also told me she was very impressed with how the dead were responding to me, and equally impressed with the messages I was recording, and asked if I would be interested in helping her work a missing teen case. I told Juli that I would think about it, and a week later I made the decision to see what I could do to help.

Juli introduced me to a person she called an advocate. The advocate, I will call her Colleen, works with different missing children and teen organizations trying through various means to find crime tip information that may help solve the crime. Colleen herself was also a former police officer who had devoted her life using her law enforcement skills to try and help find the missing.

Imagine that, here I am for my first Known Deceased Missing Person case working with two former police officers, recording Radio Sweep (Ghost Box) EVP for them with the presumed deceased crime victim. What more could I ask for?

Now up to this point my experience recording electronic voice phenomena had been phenomenal especially for a new comer to this field. Spirits were call out my first and last name, and spirits were naming items I held in my hand, so my first thought joining to help these two women was this was going to be easy. I record with the teen; he tells me where his body is; he tells me who kills him, and case closed! That my friends did not happen!

It sounds easy, but while I did get a lot of information already known by the advocate, and some key information not even the police knew, I never through the myriad of recording sessions that spanned over a period of six months receive any valid information about who did kill him or where his body was.

At the onset of this paranormal investigation, Colleen provided me the first and last name of the missing teen, and his last seen location. Juli provided me her remote view information which encompassed drawings and information she received using her mediumistic skills about the last seen location, and I then took all this information and Googled® a satellite image of the area surrounding the teen's last seen location which essentially was a gas station in a rural area surrounded by small lakes and ponds.

Since this particular case involved me recording Radio Sweep (Ghost Box) EVP over a period of six months, I will only share with you some of the questions I asked with responses, and as noted previously I will change the names of all persons involved even those mentioned in the recordings. The missing teen will be named Tom Anderson, his best friend will be named Steve Beltoy, and his fiancé will be named Sandy Jones.

At eight am sharp on April 29th 2008, I engaged a Radio Sweep (Ghost Box) EVP recording session with Tom Anderson, a teen who along with his red car had vanished without a trace. According to the advocate the boy was presumed deceased only because one of his many friends had told police he knew the boy was dead, and when police went to ask him more questions about his friend at a later date, the friend of Tom's refused to talk and had secured a lawyer. My job was to try and find the boy's body and or car which was also missing.

The first question I asked Tom was who killed him, and received a response of "Steve, Steve, Steve, I do not know". What is interesting about this message is I at the time did not know Tom's friends name. The advocate when she listened to the message told me that Steve is one of the boys that was with Tom the day he went missing.

Next I asked Tom where his body was and received a message of "Fun Field". I later learned from the advocate that Fun Field is a real place, however his body was not found there as it was found a year later on a farm ten miles from his last seen location.

Next I asked if he could say one word that if his mother or father heard it, they would know it was him, and a voice shouted out the word "water!"

So what does that mean? What does the response of water mean? Remember earlier I told you I had Googled® Tom's last seen location which was a rural area surrounded by some ponds and lakes? As I proceed with my questions during these recording sessions water was a key tip, but his body was not in it as one message seemed to indicate it was.

Just after the word water was shouted out, another voice actually shouted out my first and last name of "Mike Edwards!", so I asked if the spirit that shouted my name knew where Tom Anderson was, and I received a clear response of "Head Shot!". According to the advocate

Colleen, Tom's friend Steve had told police that Tom was shot in the head. Remember that Steve is the boy that secured a lawyer after the first interrogation, and was no longer speaking.

As I proceed through this recording session, I want to make it clear that not all these messages received were real time messages, messages that I heard clearly during the actual recording session. While I did hear my first and last name called out quite loudly, other messages I did not hear until later on play back. For this reason I continued to ask some questions over and over again, mainly because I did not know Tom had already answered them.

Next I asked Tom what color car he drove, and received a response of Red which was correct, and when I asked him what type of weapon was used to kill him, I received a response of "Gun".

Remember earlier that I told you the word water would turn out to be an important clue in this recording session. When I displayed the satellite image of his last seen location, and I asked if his body was in a field or in water, I received some real time messages of "yes" relative to the water question. Hearing these messages real time, I started to ask Tom about the two ponds behind the gas station which was his last seen location, and when I asked him if his body and car were in the big pond or the little pond, I heard a real time response of "The Little".

Now going forward, I want you to remember that response, and remember that it was a real time response, one that could be heard while I was recording and asking questions. Another thing I want you to know is at the time when I recorded this case, I was not segmenting my recorded wave files into smaller units, and I was not raising the volume of the lower sounding whisper messages that may have occurred before and after a real time message. All I did was save each question with response into its own wave file, and that file was anywhere from twenty to thirty seconds long. In today's process I allow the dead about fifteen seconds to answer.

After sharing this information with the advocate, Colleen provided me feedback on what messages were known information, and what messages had no meaning at all. She did tell me something about that little pond. This missing person case was already deemed a cold case file. The local and county police as well as the FBI had already exhausted all their resources trying to find Tom's body and or car, but during the search of that area behind the gas station, Tom's last seen location, the weather took a turn for the worse, and that particular pond was never searched.

After this initial recording session, Colleen asked me to engage another recording session with Tom to try and get more information, and on April 25th at eight AM sharp I asked Tom if he knew the name of the boy that told police he was shot in the head, and he immediately replied "Steve" which was correct.

Colleen had given me some additional information after the first recording session in that Tom and Steve had supposedly gone to meet someone the day he disappeared. Knowing this information, I asked Tom the name of the friend they went to visit and received messages that said "Wasn't good! The Gun! And it's Steve"

In one of Juli Velasquez remote view sketches, she saw what looked like a white or a grey trailer home, so I asked Tom who were they going to meet at the trailer, and I got no messages, but when I asked an additional question what the name of the road was where the trailer is, I recorded "You can go ahead and die! Receipts!"

The message receipts I want you to remember. This message turns out to be a very important tip from Tom as just after Colleen shared this information and the information about the little pond in the previous recording session with the original search and rescue coordinator, the coordinator told Colleen that the little pond was never searched due to a change in the weather.

After much discussion with Colleen, the original search and rescue coordinator secure the right permission to search that little pond and the surrounding area, and guess what she found? Surrounding the pond, she found a back of receipts, and the receipts belonged to Tom. Also in that bag was a diary which belonged to Tom's fiancé. Surrounding the pond were new tires purchased by the victim, and in the pond was a leather jacket with a comb, a wallet, and a gun with the serial numbers etched off. Upon finding these items, the coordinator called police who secured the area. No body or car was found which is what I believed would be found there based on the information in the recordings. For the next several months I continued to record with Tom documenting more information, and documenting personal messages for his mother and father. Tom's body was eventually found ten miles away from the little pond, and his killer through a tip was arrested.

After reading all of the above, and mind you the above information resulted from the first just two recording sessions, and does not include the myriad of recording sessions I engaged in with Tom over six months, why did I not record any information about where Tom's body and all cases I have recorded thus far. The dead for some unknown reason do not know where their body is. My initial thought about this was that they did know. Heck, Sam in the movie "Ghost" knew where his body was, and he knew who killed him, and where the killer lived, so why I thought does Tom not know where his body and especially his beloved red car are located. It made no sense to me, and how could it, because I have never been dead to have such an experience.

I noticed this trend in almost all my cases recording Radio Sweep (Ghost Box) EVP with the dead in that the dead did not give me any info where their body was located. They could give me details that led up to their death, how they died, what weapon was used, or even give descriptions what the person looked like that killed them, but some of them were not able to give me a body location. Of the twenty five missing person/crime cases I have recorded thus far, only four victims were able to give me their body location, and only one of the four was verified. The others like Tom Anderson could not tell me.

Frustrated, I contacted a Medium friend explaining the situations of some of my recording sessions in that the dead could in most cases tell me where their body was located. She told me her belief why some of them do not know is based on the circumstance of their death, and on what happened moments after they died. If they went to the light immediately after death, they left their body behind, and even if they remember where they were killed at, the killer may have moved the body to another location. The victim may also have been blind folded when taken to where they were killed, and as noted previously they went to the light, but in this case they do not even have a location to share with the recorder where they were killed. Severe trauma could also play a role why they do not know in that they forgot everything before their death before going to the light. If they stayed behind to watch the goings on, as did I believe one drowning victim I recorded probably did, they would know where their body was.

All of the above is something to think about if you the reader decide to record this type of session. Do not get frustrated if the dead can't or don't tell you where their body is. They may not know.

Now I can only imagine what you the reader of this book are thinking. I bet you are thinking already about starting to record Radio Sweep (Ghost Box) EVP with a Known Deceased Missing Person. I bet you are thinking based on how well I did recording my first case, even though I was unable to find Tom's body, car or even learn the name of his killer, that recording sessions of this type will be easy and rewarding. Do not believe it.

Each Known Deceased Missing Person case will be different and success will depend, I have discovered, on what background or experience and access to vital case information the person you are recording for has. For my first case, I was lucky. Both people that asked for my assistance were former police officers having knowledge how to proceed with an investigation, and the advocate, Colleen had access to information the police already knew about the case, information the general public, Tom's parents, and not even the news media knew about. Having access to this information, helped Colleen to formulate the right questions for me to ask Tom, and should he provided the correct answer, another crime puzzle piece would be fitted into place.

To help you better understand what I am trying to tell you, the next case I am about to share with you will explain it all.

The Missing Husband

So far you have read over two what I believe were good missing person cases in which using my Radio Sweep (Ghost Box) EVP process I was able to record Paranormal information known by the authorities, new information that proved fruitful, and personal information that was shared with the deceased victim. Likewise I recorded Suspect Paranormal information to which could not be readily explained.

I also explained to you that not all of these Known Deceased Missing Person cases share equal success, and some will result in no success at all.

Based on my experience thus far, people who record with a Known Deceased Missing Person or even a crime victim, in my opinion ideally they should have a law enforcement or investigator background, and they should have access to all known information the police working the case have privy to. This missing husband case will make you realized how important it is to have access to all known information the authorities have.

Right around the same time I was recording Radio Sweep (Ghost Box) EVP with the missing teen Tom Anderson, Colleen had also asked me to record with the dead to try and locate a missing husband from Nevada. He disappeared May 19th, 2005, and his wife had contacted Colleen as she had exhausted all efforts to try and find her husband who went to work one day, and never came home.

Now even though Colleen was a former police officer, and even though she had access to known information the police had in the Tom Anderson case, she did not have access to that information the Nevada police had, and her not having this information proved a disaster at least from my perspective.

Not having a Medium like Juli Velasquez to perform a remote view did not help either, so I was essentially recording blind as a bat. I did not know if this guy was dead or alive. Imagine yourself in this situation. This is your second paranormal missing person case, and the first case was such a good success with many verified hits, how in the world would this case pan out.

In all honesty, and because of Tom's case in which I was able to record valid data, I felt very confident I would be able to pull this off without a hitch! I did some research on the internet, and found a satellite image of his last seen location, and like Tom's case, I asked my guide to either find this missing husband who I will name as Derek Belcher, or to find another spirit that knew anything about Derek Belcher.

Right away when I asked if anyone knew what happened to Derek Belcher, I received a message he was dead, so hearing that real time, I asked if Derek was with me today, and received a response of "Yes".

Colleen had received information from Derek's wife that co-workers told her Derek left the office to run an errand, and had never returned. With this information, I started receiving messages that Derek had been kidnapped, taken by a woman to an undisclosed location and murdered. I also received information in which a first and last name of the woman was provided, a name I found in a Las Vegas phone book, and when I looked at this location via satellite, it was not far from where Derek had worked. How amazing is that I thought!

Believing I had something of value here, and since Juli Velasquez was not available, I contacted another Medium I met through the internet, and sent this person the satellite image of the home where the woman mentioned in the recordings lived, and the Medium said Derek's body was in the fish pond out back. Can you imagine the excitement I was experiencing from all this?

Little did I know some entity, perhaps some Dark

Head was giving me wrong information from the very start, and very soon I was sternly informed through a phone call from Colleen that Derek was identified by police as being alive, but Derek did not want the police to tell his wife and nor where he was.

What a horrible blow this was for me, but even a greater blow to Derek's wife who was being told her husband is dead, and now she finds he is alive and does not want to see her.

Have I scared you straight! Are you thinking twice about ever trying to record Radio Sweep (Ghost Box) EVP with a Known Deceased Missing Person?

I wasted three months of my life recording for information about a missing person that was already known by police. On top of that, this same false information I received from the spirit world was relayed to Colleen the advocate and thereon to Derek's wife. If Colleen had access to the known information about this case, this fiasco would not have happened.

Now imagine yourself after having just experienced a recording session as did I with the supposed missing husband Derek Belcher. If someone came to you frantically asking for your help whether they were an advocate like Colleen, or even a family member of the missing person or crime victim, would you even after this horrible experience you just encountered, record with the victim, not having any information the police already know? You probably would if you care about people, and I did, and I have continued to try and help with cases some of which I still experience same or similar nice scenarios as with Tom Anderson, and I still experience fruitless scenarios much like the supposed missing husband recording session.

The only difference between new cases I have recorded since the supposed missing husband Derek Belcher is I now inform family members that have come directly to me, and I also inform advocates that have come directly to me, that some of the information or even all of the information recorded could be wrong and not from the victim. Dark Heads could give false information, or while I am recording with their loved one or the victim, other dead watching the recording session could be having side conversations with each other as they watch the recording session, and their messages will get picked up by the recorder.

So why am I telling you about my bad cases, you may ask. If I only told you about my good cases, I would be doing you a great disservice giving you a false impression every case recorded with a Known Deceased Missing Person or a crime victim will yield valid results. I do not want any reader of this book to follow the same path that I did making the same mistakes, mistakes that can hurt unsuspecting people should they see or hear any wrong information received especially when they are not expecting such could occur.

The next case is about an eleven year old boy that vanished without a trace in the state of Washington, USA. I recorded this case for a friend that was curious about what I would find, and while I did eventually mail the information from the recording session to the local police chief, no one has contacted me for further information. This particular case is one I am hoping will get solved soon.

The Missing Eleven Year Old Boy

For this particular case, like the Tom Anderson case, I knew of information the police already know. Please note, the names of all those involved in this case, have been changed to help protect their identity.

Calvin Bison was eleven years old, living with his father and his father's live in girlfriend Carley. Calvin disappeared September 2004. When I first recorded with Calvin, I began to receive messages from him that he was killed by a man named Walter. Please note at this time, I was not using the file segmentation and transcription process I use today. Back then, I literally recorded twenty to thirty second files that consisted of a question with an answer, whereas today, I slice up the recorded question with answer file into multiple files, so I can hear all the lower sounding words, sentences and or phrases that may occur before or after a real time sounding message.

It was after I had established my current process that I went back and used it on cases that had yet to be resolved. I ran this new process against all the Calvin Bison files, and found I had missed a lot of information that was recorded before and after the real time messages in the files. The messages transcribed proved to be more in line with what law enforcement already knew, but still it was not enough or even believable enough to cause a stir in law enforcement that were originally involved in the case. This was a cold case, and the authorities believe the boy's father killed him; however, the information I heard after using my new process indicates the father was not directly involved.

The following are questions I asked Calvin, with answers using my current process I use today which is described in this book. Remember I have changed the names of all those mentioned in this case and the recorded messages to protect their identity.

I asked if this boy Calvin Bison is here today, and received several responses each recorded and saved in the order in which they were recorded.

- Then he threw his glasses at me
- They killed me
- He murdered Calvin
- And called to death, takes the highway.

Next I asked who killed Calvin, and received the following two responses.

- They lock the bedroom
- Stepmom

Next I asked Calvin to tell me the location where he was murdered, and received the following messages.

- Then you throw the salad on me
- She is shouting! Do you want it!

Next I asked Calvin "And if you are here. I don't know if you are or not. Can you please stand right next to me and look at this satellite image of xyz city, WA the town you live in", and I received a response of the following two messages.

- Murdered it was Michael
- That's our city!

What is really interesting with that last response, is I had displayed on my computer the Google® Earth satellite image of his city he lived in when he went missing.

Next I asked Calvin if his body was buried anywhere there, meaning in the satellite image displayed on my computer, and I received a response of "Hurt him, it was his cousin".

Next I asked Calvin if his body was on land or in water, and received a message of "My friend me. He prayed. Brian saw me"

I asked him the same question again, and received responses as follows.

- They were so happy I miss the party, but guess who see her
- This aint the deal!
- He was the one who get me
- The back seat! This is what you want to see! The back seat!

Next I asked Calvin "Calvin if you are standing right now on top of where your body is at, what can you see around you", and I received the following messages.

- I was his son, and they kill me
- He saw them in the bedroom, then I must die
- His father did not. He's praying for Calvin

Next I ask "If Calvin is dead and he is here right now, do you have any messages for your sisters please say it now", and I received the following responses.

- He loved his dad
- He used to play with me
- Before she had to wait on his kids
- They are kissing
- Took it slow in the bedroom
- Feels away you loved him back
- I am running fast to the "?"
- He said what are you going to make of this? I saw you kissing in the bedroom
- In our father's kitchen stabbing me

What is really amazing is some of this info about

the kitchen has proven quite interesting, but most people if not all I have spoken to believe the boy was killed by his authoritarian father. The recordings, however, tell a tale the boy walked on his step mom with another man, and that man is the one who killed Calvin.

As seen in the Missing Husband case, this information may be false info from another spirit, or it could be valid information that has yet to be verified. If Calvin's father is innocent based on what these recordings reveal, I pray to God and to Jesus Christ Calvin's father learns the truth and gives his son a proper burial.

With this case I know some of the information is valid, at least from the kitchen perspective, but as for the rest of the information, it is nowhere close to what the locals in that area have determined in their minds as to what actually happened to this young man. As with any case I record, I hope to learn the truth and see Calvin get the proper burial he deserves.

For this last and final Known Deceased Missing Person case I am about to share with you, it is actually a crime case in which the person that is missing is the murderer. This case is on one of the FBIs most wanted list. As noted previously, all names have been changed to protect the identity, in this case however, of the remaining living family.

One of the FBI's Most Wanted

In the year 2008, after reviewing the FBIs most wanted list, I came across a case in which a man murdered his wife and his children, and thereafter blew up their home with explosives. For purposes of this case, I will name his wife Rachel whom I recorded and documented thirty eight Radio Sweep (Ghost Box) EVP files with on September 10 and 12, 2008. This case was and still is one of the most disturbing crime cases I have ever recorded, and it haunts me to this day. I mailed all my recorded information to the FBI, and have received no response. In truth, I can only imagine they probably thought I was a nut job, and trashed what I sent them.

If I was an FBI agent at the time I recorded with Rachel, I would have tried to resolve the case, and I believe there is information I recorded that could solve this case, and my belief is based purely on intuition. It is my hope some open minded law enforcement professional will read this book, and put two and two together, and figure out what criminal this case refers to, and thereon follow up on what I have recorded.

I remember vividly when I first recorded with Rachel, I had told her I would help her solve her case, and sadly I failed her. I was so confident back then. Since there are so many recorded files associated with this case, I will only share key files. My sole intent recording with Rachel was to see if she knew the physical location where her fugitive husband was living, so I could alert the authorities.

On September 10, 2008 just after I asked Rachel "Can you find your husband's location right now, so he won't do to others what he did to her and their children. Do you know where he is living right now?", I received the following responses.

- It is laboratories
- He is a lab boy
- Basic business and he tests
- He was a lab boy first
- First he must breast feed them
- He gets awful scratches
- Be at girls house parents of Lisa
- Parents house is now available

Next I asked Rachel if her husband was using a different name, and she responded with a name that phonetically sounded like "Paul Jason Arden".

During the September 12 2008 recording with Rachel, when I asked her what city her husband was living in right now, she said "Atlanta", and later when I asked her what city and state her husband was living in, I recorded a message of "First they move to Hill Street, and he bought five homes. He wouldn't stop buying. He's a monster. By the name of Jesse, first class. He bought her and gave the keys to her. Once he calls her dumb. The first books fail. Her first own book"

When I asked her yet again if she could tell me the first and last name her husband was using, she said "He sneaks in the closet church room and waits for the priest to fill the bag. Number to remember 44537. This is his number"

Next, when I asked the same question again, I recorded "The FBI is watching his house, but it wasn't his. Today he is use and on a priest. They say running better was 44537"

When I said thanks to Rachel for coming, she said "It is your city in 44537. Friends he has are millionaires".

Now this was an amazing case, and I only shared with you some key files I felt had meaning. Initially I thought that the numbers 44537 were related to a zip code, however, when I Googled® 44537 the results yielded an Ohio Zip Code, but also building addresses. Due to my not being a law enforcement professional, I have no clue what 44537 means in this case, but it surely must have meaning as it was repeated in the recording more than once.

If the above information is valid from Rachel, I am

truly saddened that the FBI did not look into this information I sent them, but at the same time I can understand why they probably trashed it. Again and as mentioned before, it is my hope someone reading this book will know what case I am talking about, and they will follow up and see if the information recorded ties to the FBIs top ten most wanted family murderer.

In closing this section of Chapter Twelve, my recommendation to each of you reading this book, if any of you decide to try and record Radio Sweep (Ghost Box) EVP or even traditional recorder only EVP with a Known Deceased Missing Person or even a crime victim case, please consider the following.

- Ideally the recorder should have a law enforcement background, and have access to information the police working the case already know.
- Record for advocates that do have access to what police already know
- If you record for a family member of the victim, make it very clear some or even all of the information recorded may be false information given by a dark Head or other spirits listening in.
- If at all possible do not record and give recorded results to a family member of the victim.

Paranormal Investigation Cases

Unlike recording with a Known Deceased Person one in which all messages received are initially classified as Suspect Paranormal until the client can validate messages as having any meaning, the Paranormal Investigation Cases are similar to recording with a Known Deceased Missing Person in that information about the crime, the victim or the site being investigated may already be known allowing the person who listens to and transcribes the Radio Sweep (Ghost Box) EVP recording to classify a message straight away as being Paranormal.

To help you understand what to expect during a recording session of this type, I have outlined some of my most interesting paranormal investigations I was able to participate in using my Shack Hack 12-469 Radio Sweep (Ghost Box) EVP device.

Ferry Plantation Home – Virginia Beach, Virginia

The Ferry Plantation Home paranormal investigation was my first to attend just after having joined a local paranormal Meet-Up group, The Carolina Haunting, Apparitions and Poltergeists Society http://www.meetup.com/Carolina-Paranormal/. I attended this meet-up at Ferry Plantation with a group of about 16 paranormal enthusiasts from the Raleigh, North Carolina area January 10, 2009.

George Matthis runs this local meet up group which is managed by staff from NSPIR (National Society of Paranormal Investigation and Research, Inc on facebook®. He had given me permission to use my device along with my digital recorder. Members of his group and nor his staff had ever used nor seen a Radio Sweep (Ghost Box) EVP device, and they preferably use the digital recorder only to record for paranormal messages from the dead.

From a historical perspective through direct quote from the Ferry web page http://www.ferryplantation.org/about/brief-history.html

"Ferry plantation first got its name in 1642 when the Ferry Boat Service ran the Lynnhaven waterway, as far as we have traced back there may have been as many as eleven stops along the river. The ferry operator was summoned by a signal cannon, one at each of the eleven stops. Three of these cannons have been located. Saville Gaskin was the ferry operator, in 1642 he was commissioned by Adam Thoroughgood.

The Ferry Landing had been chosen because the land had already been cleared by native Indian tribe in the 1500's. Many Indian artifacts have been found on the Plantation that further tell the story of her past.

The second Princess Anne court house was built on the Plantation near the present location of Old Donation Church , this was the courthouse that held part of the trial of Grace Sherwood, Virginia's only convicted with that was tried by water and found guilty of witchcraft, Grace was jailed for some time in this timber courthouse . The trial took place on July 10th 1706, at that time the church that was used , built in 1692 was the Brick Church , this was outgrown and was replaced with the church that stands on that location today It was completed in 1736.

The third Princess Anne Courthouse was built in 1735 of brick on Ferry Plantation to replace the timber courthouse. This was built closer to the Ferry Landing. This courthouse was used until 1751, the stocks and pillory were taken from Ferry Plantation in 1751 to the new courthouse location at Newtown. The Walke family owning the property at that time built the Manor house , there have been several dig sites open for the public to see the remains of the past, and telling our family history.

In 1828 the Walke Manor house burned to the ground. It was not until two years later 1830 that George and Elizabeth (Walke) MacIntosh built from the good bricks of the manor house the house that stands on the Plantation today. It was built for their seventeen year old son Charles Fleming MacIntosh."

As you can see this house is rich in history, and I will tell you through firsthand experience Ferry Plantation Home is indeed haunted. I found it to be a very active house filled with kind and loving spirits who seemed happy to have us visit with them.

Several days before my arrival, I said prayers to my guardian angel to inform any dead that hang out at Ferry Plantation that I was coming. I also asked my guide to explain to the deceased inhabitants that I would have a Radio Sweep (Ghost Box) EVP device with me, and if the conditions were right, the dead at Ferry could speak to me real time, meaning that I would be able to hear them, and I would be able to talk back to them with a response. During this particular paranormal investigation, I classified all messages received as Paranormal.

After we arrived, the group of sixteen was split up into two groups of eight. One group would take photographs and record EVP in every room downstairs, while the other group would do the same up-stairs. Group leaders communicated to each other using two way radios.

In each room our group visited, our group leader, Jeremy Mullins, would start off the EVP session using what I call the traditional device, a digital recorder, and each person would ask questions of the dead that may be in the room with us. After so many minutes, the group leader would then allow me to use my Shack Hack 12-469 Radio Sweep (Ghost Box) EVP device to ask questions.

When I turned my device on for the first time in our first room, and asked if there were any dead in the room with us, we all heard a real time message that said "Yes!" Next I asked the dead in our room to count out how many of us were in the room, and we heard a real time message of eight which was correct.

By now everyone in our group were so hooked on using the Shack Hack device that we discontinued using the traditional "recorder only" method through the remainder of the house. This house was very active, and hearing their real time messages was giving us all one heck of a thrill!

In practically every room in the house I would ask what holiday the dead in the room liked, and we heard real time messages of "Christmas", and then when we were in the last room before we quit for the night, I asked why they liked Christmas so much, and we got a real time message that said "because of the presents".

In another room, I asked what happened to the slaves by the old tree out back, and we received a real time message that said "they were hung".

All throughout the house we experienced real time messages, but later on play back, I also learned other EVP we did not hear real time was also picked up by the recorder.

In the kitchen area of the home, for example, which is actually where the fireplace is, I asked two questions that were recorded from the dead. I asked the dead what color shirt Jeremy Mullins was wearing, and got a message of "Red" which was correct. I also asked the dead to tell me what kind of animal came through the fireplace at night, and got a message of Opossum which was also correct.

In another room there was a female investigator that was pregnant, and she asked the dead to tell her if she was going to have a boy or a girl, and we got a message of Girl. This woman at the time did not know what sex her child would be, but when I contacted her after her due date, she informed me she indeed did have a baby girl.

In another room, we asked the dead to name each of

us, and for some we got real time messages, one being Boris, and another being Tikki which are unique names and correct responses. As you can imagine we were all so amazed at what we were hearing which egged us on to ask more questions.

In one room we learned from the house manager of a little girl that supposedly hung out in the room we were in, and when we asked how old she was, we got a message of "Just six". To listen to my recordings from Ferry Plantation Home, feel free to join my Yahoo® web group at http://tech.groups.yahoo.com/group/EVP-ITC-SDWR-SpeakingToTheDeadWithRadios-/?yguid=338683728, or listen to some of my videos on You Tube® at my channel EVPITCSDWR.

All in all recording Radio Sweep (Ghost Box) EVP during a paranormal investigation, under the right conditions can be quite enjoyable especially if members hear real time messages. What is important to remember is you need to ask permission of the group leaders before you start using the device as some members may not want you to use it.

The Earl Webb Library – Morehead City, NC

On March 20th, 2010, I was invited to participate in another overnight paranormal investigation, but this time at the Earl Webb Library in Morehead City, NC with the Carolina Hauntings, Apparitions and Poltergeists Society. George Matthis as noted previously is the founder of this group who had authorized me to use my Radio Sweep (Ghost Box) EVP device during the investigation along with others in attendance who were just using digital recorders only.

From a historical perspective noted at this URL, http://www.thewebblibrary.com/webb-history.htm, through direct quote

"In 1929 Mr. Earle W. Webb, Sr., CEO of Ethyl Corporation in NYC and native Morehead City resident, began construction of a commercial building on the corner of 9th and Evans Streets in downtown Morehead City, North Carolina.

For the first few years the building had doctor's offices downstairs and a training facility for the local garment factory upstairs. When the upstairs noise became too much for the downstairs occupants the garment factory left.

Mrs. Webb, a member of the Morehead Woman's Club, asked her husband if the club could move its 300 book library to one of the upstairs rooms. When he agreed the library was moved.

A few years later, in 1936, the Webb's son, Earle W. Webb, Jr. became ill and died. In honor of their son, Mr. and Mrs. Webb dedicated the building as the Earle W. Webb Jr. Memorial Library and Civic Center and opened it to all the citizens of Morehead City for community use.

In 2003 the trust supporting the facility was no longer viable. At that time several interested citizens petitioned the town of Morehead City for help and the town council agreed to help with the day to day costs while a steering committee researched level of interest in the community to maintain a library and gathering place for it's citizens. The steering committee recommended that the town take over full support of the library and in 2007 the town and the Webb family agreed on terms that would allow the town to keep the library and the building.

Today the building is more familiarly called The Webb and provides services for locals and visitors from all over North Carolina and beyond. The book collection has grown to over 11,000 books and there are 7 public use computers. In August 2009, the library celebrated its 75th year of service to the public."

At eight PM we arrived and met the overnight library manager who would stay with us and escort us throughout the library during the overnight hours of our investigation. The manager laid out the ground rules, and walked us through each room telling us tales of past investigators or visitors to the library. Previous reports revealed the ghostly apparition of a fisherman walking through the library, and of a spirit that moves books out of place sometimes stacking them one on top the other during the overnight hours only to be discovered the next day.

The night before the investigation, I had said some prayers and asked my Guardian Angel to inform the spirits that hung out in the library that I was coming to visit them, and that I would have a hacked radio that under the right conditions while it was scanning stations, I would be able to hear the dead speak real time through the noise of the radio. Additionally, I also asked my guide to invite my wife's recently deceased grandmother to attend the investigation with me.

To those of you reading this book who have never seen on television or have never attended a paranormal investigation before, there are generally two teams combing the location using cameras and recording equipment to record voices of the dead or capture paranormal anomalies on film, an apparition for example, and both teams communicate with each other using two way radios. Those manning the radios are generally group leaders who signal to the other leader they are about to engage their investigation of a particular floor or room at the location. Once both teams are in place, one usually upstairs or outside, and the other downstairs or outside, the leaders start their clock ending their investigation at a set time, and thereon informing the other team using the two way radio they have completed their investigation, and are now moving to the next location. These start and stop communications are repeated over and over until all intended rooms or areas are investigated by both teams.

Within each of these rooms or locations, the team leads will allow each person to ask questions of the dead that may be in that room to try and capture any paranormal messages on their recorders, or capture any anomalies on their cameras.

After the investigation of the location has been completed, all equipment is stored away in their vehicles, and attendees return home to listen to what they recorded and/or review their film for any paranormal anomalies.

Depending on the organization, all recording and film that has been analyzed will be discussed at a set meeting, and if this particular investigation is of the type for an actual client, the group leaders will meet with the client, and review what they found.

For this particular investigation at the Earle Webb Library, this was actually a Meet-Up investigation one in which weekend paranormal enthusiast meet on set dates to participate in an investigation hosted by a professional paranormal investigation team. This team generally teaches the weekend enthusiast, or Meet-Up members how they perform an actual investigation at let's say a client's home or location. The Meet-Up investigation occurs in a more relaxed setting one in which the members can enjoy and at the same time learn from the professionals.

After the library tour, the lights were turned off

leaving the library pitch black, and all twelve of us split into teams of six sending some to the basement and ground floor, while the others went to the second floor of the library.

In the basement when it came to my turn to ask questions of any dead in the room, I noticed right away that the Radio Sweep (Ghost Box) EVP device I was using, a hacked Radio Shack® model 12-469 radio was not getting any reception, and therefore I had to shut down, and just use my digital recorder. I experienced this once before when trying to use the device inside the Battleship North Carolina. Like the steel walls of the ship, the brick walls of the basement would not allow any reception to get through rendering the device useless under those conditions.

On the first floor while I did get good radio reception, I did not record any suspect or paranormal messages there. It was on the second floor in the storeroom across from the Classic reading room, and the other room to the right of the storeroom that I recorded suspect and paranormal messages.

In the storeroom which was a bit crowded, the team lead allowed each Meet-Up member to ask questions of the dead just using recorders only, and then toward the last ten minutes the team lead allowed me to use my Radio Sweep (Ghost Box) EVP device. Almost instantly after turning the radio on to scan mode a real time voice shouted out a Meet-Up member's name, Farrah!

Farrah being so excited by this Paranormal message, she proceeded to ask other questions as did other members. When it came my turn to ask if there were any dead that knew me in the room, a real time voice said "Iappa is here with you". In total shock by what I heard others in the room had no idea the meaning to which I explained that was the name of my wife's grandmother whom I asked my guardian angel to invite to attend the investigation with me. I classified both of these messages as Paranormal.

After moving to the next room to the right of the storeroom, a room that appeared to be a children's book room with a piano, when it was my turn to ask questions, I asked "Is the person that knocks down the books are you here right now?" and recorded a response of "I told you! Bullshit!" For this particular message I classified it as Suspect Paranormal. I am confident it is not radio traffic because radio announcers nor guests are allowed to use profane words during a radio show, and even if they do, the station bleeps them out, but I am not sure it is Paranormal.

Next I asked "Can you whistle for us", and I recorded a Paranormal response of "He's asking you to whistle". While we never heard a whistle real time or even on play back, the fact we recorded that response indicates to me an intelligent spirit was there among us.

Lastly, and after asking again "Is the person that knocks down the books are you here right now?", I recorded two responses, each saved into their own wave files.

- Yes, he's in front of you
- He has a lot of family. I miss my mom

The Granger Hill Performing Arts Center – Kinston, NC
On August 28th, 2010 I attend another paranormal investigation with the Carolina Hauntings, Apparitions and Poltergeists Society of Raleigh, NC. This investigation was at the historic Granger Hill Performing Arts Center in

Kinston, NC. Thirteen members of this Meet-Up group attended, and after the ground rules were set, two groups were assembled of six and seven each with a group leader and a two way radio.

From a historical perspective, and by direct quote from this URL, http://www.meetup.com/Carolina-Paranormal/events/14397646/

"Listed in the National Historic Register, the former Grainger High School in Kinston, North Carolina is one of the last remaining examples of Greek Classical Revival Architecture still standing in North Carolina. It was constructed in 1925 for $555,000 as a three-story school, auditorium and gymnasium complex capable of housing 900 students. Thousands of students passed through its doors during the 69 years it was used as a public school. In December of 1987 students were reassigned to other facilities and the complex was retired.

Rumors of paranormal activity have circulated since the 1970's, focused primarily on the auditorium area of the school. Reports of touches, cold spots, hearing voices, open windows that were left closed, and small pieces of brick being thrown at people on the catwalk above the stage are just some of the unusual activities that have taken place. "

Due to the size and area of this complex, a walk through tour was only provided to the team leads. Everyone entered the building from the back stage entrance, and met on stage to discuss the rules for the evening and to split up into teams.

My team was the first to climb up to the catwalk area which is where previous visitors have reported pieces of brick were thrown down at them. After each member asked their questions using their recorders, I was allowed to use my Radio Sweep (Ghost Box) EVP device to ask questions of any dead that may be lurking on that catwalk.

Just after I asked if there were any dead in the catwalk with us, I recorded a message that said "Mike I'm with you", and the word Mike was heard real time by me and another member. Since my name of Mike was mentioned, and the message said I'm with you, I classified this message as Paranormal because I feel the message was directed at me.

As noted above, one of the other members heard the word Mike, and he asked "who said Mike's name", and I recorded a response of "I did! And we know you can hear me, and he spoke for me". For this message since I felt it was referring directly to me, and since the spirit responded "I did" when asked who said my name, I classified this message as Paranormal.

The next message recorded just after the above said "Tell him that Madeline is in love with you". For this message I classified it as Suspect Paranormal as I could not determine who it was directed to, but it could be the spirits name was Madeline, and she was saying she was in love with me, or it could also have been radio traffic. I, however, am more willing to believe it is Suspect Paranormal and not radio traffic at all.

After leaving the cat-walk area, we all moved down into the basement area to which my radio sweep device did not get enough reception and proved useless to capture any messages there. One member did however experience a sort of pass-through experience by an entity in the basement with such a force she was thrown to the floor in front of all of us! She was so frightened and shaken that it took her a while to regain her composure before were able to move back upstairs.

Chapter Thirteen:
The Applications are Endless

From reading this book, you have learned about the history of Radio Sweep (Ghost Box) Electronic Voice Phenomena, you have learned how I speak to the dead with radios; you have learned about the best radios to hack, and you have learned what you seek you will find in terms of both negative and positive spirits. You have also learned how to prepare for your first recording with the dead, how to record with the dead, how to upload and convert your files, how to listen to and transcribe them, and lastly you have learned how to prepare your recorded files and transcriptions for yourself or for a client.

Within three years time I have learned and developed what I deem is an exceptional Radio Sweep (Ghost Box) EVP recording and transcription process of the type "Show and They Tell", "Deceased Loved One", "Known Deceased Missing Person", and "Paranormal Investigations" each of which continue to evolve as I learn better methods and processes.

The applications are endless my friends relative to what each of you can use Radio Sweep (Ghost Box) EVP devices for. What is next from this point forward is strictly up to you, but it is my hope you will take this process tweaking it as necessary, and use Radio Sweep (Ghost Box) EVP devices as a tool to record information from the dead, information that may facilitate life and perhaps help change the world in good ways never even imagined.

Futurists

Not long ago, I was having a conversation with a friend about an organization whose members peer into what they call parallel universes using the process of remote viewing to learn about technologies these parallel universes have that would be or could become new and feasible technology here in our own time. He told me he heard some of these people that call themselves "Futurists" were being paid high salaries by mid to large companies and corporations to try and find out what would be considered in our time as new breakthrough technologies present day companies and corporations could design, develop and deploy in today's markets.

Hearing about these Futurist organizations got me thinking. What if a Futurist reads this book, and what if they decide rather than use remote viewing or the process of data mining alone, they add my Radio Sweep (Ghost Box) EVP process to their arsenal of discovery tools to record with a spirit that has knowledge of these parallel universes and what their technology is compared to ours? The Futurist could make an appointment through their guide or guardian angel to find and contact a deceased person that actually died after having lived in one of these parallel universes. If this deceased person or spiritual entity can relay descriptions of their technology and how it works, companies and corporations contracting these Futurists here present day Earth may be able to design, develop, and deploy this technology which may help make our world a better place.

Do you see where I am going with this dialog? This book is not just for weekend paranormal enthusiast, existing Radio Sweep (Ghost Box) EVP enthusiast, or even average people that are out searching the internet trying find a way to make contact with their loved ones, it is also for people like the Futurists that also want to find ways to improve our future and the way we live.

Not sure how you feel, but I am one of those people that believe certain dead know the answers to all questions we have, and if we can reach them, they will if they are authorized to do so, share those answers. I also believe these same dead or entities currently plant thoughts and ideas in our heads to help us discover or invent.

Am I a dreamer? Perhaps I am, but I do know I and any person out there can communicate with the dead using hacked radios and recorders, and for any person to have that ability, especially those persons that want to know the answers to all their questions, having this access will allow them to ask, receive, document, and proceed toward getting answers for their next unanswered question. Google® or Bing® are tools none of us had access to not long ago, which give us access to seek out answers to questions we need answers to, and the spirit world is also a rarely tapped search engine, one which can become available to the masses, to every person on this planet, to seek out answers to life's age old questions and a whole lot more.

To access this search engine, however, people need a tool, they need a search engine, and in my opinion that search engine is using Radio Sweep (Ghost Box) EVP devices along with recording devices, and using transcription processes like mine of which is available present day while you read this book. Soon hereafter other new and more finely tuned processes designed and deployed to the world by others will become available.

The Age of Ethereal Connection

Remember earlier I mentioned I believe present day Earth is entering a new age. I believe we are all entering what I call "The Age of Ethereal Connection", an age in which the veil that now separates most of us from our family, friends, religious leaders, and spiritual beings is being pierced with a direct link that will allow communication unlike anything we have ever known or experienced. This link through the veil, in my opinion, is the telephone to the dead, it is the search engine that will help us connect to find answers to our questions, answers that can be formulated into actions to facilitate life and help unite everyone in the physical realm to work with each other toward a common goal of acceptance, tolerance, peace and love. Those of us that reach these goals before passing on to the ethereal world will be ready for our next mission.

What areas of our life living as doctors, lawyers, dentists, medical researchers, mechanical engineers, electrical engineers, industrial engineers, civil engineers, aeronautical, space, and automotive engineers, software engineers, teachers, religious leaders, ship builders, construction builders, road builders, chemists, botanists, geneticists, scientists, etc… can be improved in addition to unite each of us toward a common goal? If each of you who belong to any one of the above vocations listed or others not listed were to think of ways to improve those vocations, to reinvent existing processes or invent new processes, you

174

would come up with a huge list which I am sure would yield many questions with answers thereafter that would turn into actions that would turn into inventions or improvements.

While it is true we can obtain many of our much needed answers through data mining existing data or through think tanks, it is those questions present day we have no answers for that can be presented as a question through the veil for answers. These questions, however, in my opinion must be asked by those holding degrees and experience in the field of study they need answers for.

Present day AIDS researchers can record using Radio Sweep (Ghost Box) EVP technology to record answers they have how to prevent AIDS, what causes it to happen in the first place, and how to cure it. They can try and contact a known deceased researcher, or try and contact a researcher from a parallel universe that knows the answer to these questions.

A volcanologist can record with a deceased volcanologist from our world, or with one who passed from a parallel universe to try and find out how to accurately predict when an eruption will occur resulting in saved lives.

Present day earth quake specialists can do the same trying to find out how to accurately predict when an earth quake will occur which again will result in saved lives.

Scientists can record to ask what pollution free fuels are being used present day in a parallel universe that can be used today, so we can refit and clean up our air and waterways. Even if parallel universes do not exist, some deceased person or entity may know the answer to that question.

Climatologists can record with the dead to try and

find out how to positively affect the weather to rain on certain drought stricken areas. Perhaps climatologists that have passed from our world now know the answer to this question, or perhaps a climatologist from a parallel universe knows how to cause rain to occur.

How many readers of this book watch Star Trek®? How many of you would rather have a transporter room in your home to transport you to the mall, the grocery store, to a vacation spot or even to work? Think about how clean the air would be if everyone had a transporter room. No more trains, no more cars, no more trucks, planes or boats, heck no more noise pollution let alone air pollution. Now what if you are a scientific researcher in this field of study, and you read this book, and you decide to try and connect with let's say a deceased entity that passed into Heaven from a parallel universe that has and has used transporter technology. Imagine that this entity over some amount of time shares with you the formula to design, develop and deploy a transporter. Matthew 7:7 Ask and it shall be given you.

If we do not ask, we will never know the answer to our questions, and what I just said is a true statement. To those of us that currently record Radio Sweep (Ghost Box) EVP with the dead, we need to steer ourselves in a direction to start using the device as a tool to get answers to questions that when answered, can make a difference, and we also should be steering newcomers to this field of study to do the same.

For the future, I envision readers of this book who perhaps are established paranormal investigators wanting to learn more about radio sweep technology and how it can fit into their process, current radio sweep enthusiast who want to learn a new process to help them better understand what the dead are telling us, newcomers that now have an interest in the paranormal after watching the various paranormal shows on television or cable, and I also envision other people who have never taken an interest in the paranormal especially taken an interest in perhaps how Electronic Voice Phenomena devices can be used to record messages from the dead that can help facilitate life on earth, and perhaps help change the world through newly discovered cures and inventions.

Throughout my entire life thus far, I have always wondered how great inventors came up with their ideas, and/or how great scientists or medical professionals came up with new breakthrough processes and cures. I personally believe these ideas come to us from the dead, and I believe certain spirits know the answers to all questions providing these much needed answers by thought to people working toward finding the answer. Success comes when those who pick up on these thoughts or perhaps telepathic messages from the dead, and take the idea to the next level and design and deploy these breakthroughs.

I truly believe this theory as I have experienced it myself, and if you think about it yourself, I am willing to bet you can bring to mind several situations in which you too have received an idea how to solve a problem from that little voice in your head.

Imagine beyond what has just been discussed, if through every media outlet available around the world if every person watching the news, cable television or regular television heard about this book. Imagine one of these people is a police detective in any country frustrated trying to solve their case with no success. Imagine one if these police detectives reading this book, and thereon procuring the necessary equipment and recording with the known deceased crime victim to try and get the missing pieces to the puzzle they need to solve the case, and then imagine the detective either through one or more recording sessions, recording the answer that helps solve the case. It can happen and those with an open mind and a little bit of patience can take this process to the next level tweaking it and making it work to yield results.

Imagine a NASA engineer recording with other deceased engineers, and after one or more recording sessions he or she formulate a space craft design that can leave and enter the earth's atmosphere with no use of rocket propulsion.

Imagine religious leaders the likes of Clerics, Priests, Preachers, Deacons, Rabbis, or even Buddhist Monks recording with their deceased predecessors to gain knowledge and guidance how to bring about world peace and tolerance.

All of the above can be achieved by persons with open minds and great perseverance especially if there is any truth that certain dead know the answers to all things and are willing to share this information.

In closing this final chapter, I ask each of you with an open mind to embrace the concept and processes of the Radio Sweep (Ghost Box) Electronic Voice Phenomena process I have outlined here and move them forward building better devices and user friendly processes in which all people from all nations can connect with their loved ones as well as to connect with other loving beings that can help all of us on this planet live and work together in peace.

I ask that all radio electronic manufacturers, like Radio Shack® for example, please join the movement and build and make available worldwide Radio Sweep (Ghost Box) EVP devices to help ensure every person on this planet who wants to try and make contact, can using your equipment. Please ensure any person in any country can buy these devices in any of your stores, and if no store is available in their country, please ensure these people can buy the device through an on-line catalog.

I want to thank all of the pioneers of Radio Sweep (Ghost Box) Electronic Voice Phenomena who have contributed to this book, like Steve Hultay, Bruce Halliday, Frank Sumption, Joe Cioppi, Mike Coletta, Christopher Moon, and Juli Velazquez each who have shared and continue to share their knowledge and technique in building or even hacking radios to record Radio Sweep (Ghost Box) EVP

I also want to give special mention to some very talented Radio Sweep (Ghost Box) EVP researchers and enthusiast I have made new friendships through The Worldwide Radio Sweep - Ghost Box EVP Alliance group on face book®, namely Orion Silverstar, Martin Danja Bravo, Salo Stanley, Saleire's Artwork, Janet Passemore, Ed Ezra, Tim Woolworth, Spirit Medium Ursula Kalin, Neil Crosby, Jon Farrell, Lance Reed, Alicia Perry, Lisa Feoranz, Adriana Jones, Steve and Brandon Huff, Matthew Parker, Margaret Downey, Rob Smith, J.D. Foreman, Tracy Hultay, Andrew Openlander, Debbie Reynolds Helms, and Pat Morelli. Best wishes to each of you in recording, hacking radios, building new radios, developing better processes, and teaching and helping other people worldwide to make contact!

To each of you who have read this book, if you remember anything about listening to and transcribing paranormal messages recorded using Radio Sweep (Ghost Box) EVP technology, please remember to isolate, listen to and transcribe all the messages that occur before and after your recorded real time messages.

Finally, thanks in advance to thank all of you who will contribute to this field of study long after I am gone, and please note that someday and someday soon it is my belief we will all have a real telephone to the dead!

Credits:

Cioppi Sr., Joseph A. - Founder. Web site
www.freewebs.com/joecioppi

Clear Voice®
http://www.digitalriver.com/dr/v2/ec_MAIN.Entry10?PN=
1&SP=10023&V1=298462&xid=22766&CID=137485&C
UR=840&DSP=&PGRP=0&ABCODE=&CACHE_ID=0

Coletta, Mike - Founder. Web site
http://www.ufogeek.com/

The Ferry Plantation House. Web site
http://ferryplantation.org/

Free Audio Editor® software is copyright ©. Web site
http://free-audio-editor.com/

Gulka, Gary. Web site http://www.pro-
measure.com/P_SB7_SB7_Spirit_Box_s/98.htm

Halliday, Bruce - Founder. Web site
http://tech.groups.yahoo.com/group/inside_the_box_rtsc_g
host_box_research/

Hultay, Steve - Founder. Web site
http://tech.groups.yahoo.com/group/RTSC/, and
http://keyportparanormal.com/

Matthis, George - Founder. Web site
http://www.meetup.com/Carolina-Paranormal/

Microsoft ® is copyright© Web site
http://www.microsoft.com/en-us/default.aspx

Moon, Christopher - Founder. Web site
http://www.chrismoonpsychic.com/Chris_Moon_Psychic/H
ome.html, and
http://www.hauntedtimes.com/chrismoon.html

Mullins, Jeremy - Organizer. Web site
http://www.meetup.com/Carolina-Paranormal/

NCH Software® is copyright ©. Web site.
http://www.nch.com.au/switch/index.html

Speech Technology Center® software is copyright ©. Web
site http://speechpro.com/

Sumption, Frank - Founder. Web site
http://tech.groups.yahoo.com/group/EVP-
ITC/?yguid=338683728

Velazquez, Juli – Medium. Web site
http://www.myspace.com/462582398

About the Author:

Michael Hobert Edwards is married with two children, and lives in Cary, North Carolina. All his life he has been fascinated with the paranormal reading a variety of books on the subject, watching television shows and videos as well as engaging the subject first hand at home or with fellow paranormal enthusiasts during paranormal investigations.

In February of 2008, Michael was introduced to Radio Sweep (Ghost Box) Electronic Voice Phenomena which employs the use of an AM or FM radio both digital, or manual sweep used in conjunction with a digital or tape recorder to capture recorded messages from the dead. Michael along with a growing worldwide movement records paranormal messages from the dead to try and get answers to questions, to learn more about the spirit world, and to relay any messages from the dead back to their loved ones.

To Contact the Author:

If you wish to contact the author or would like more information about this book, please contact the author directly through his Yahoo® web group EVP-ITC-SDWR-Speaking to the Dead with Radios at this URL http://tech.groups.yahoo.com/group/EVP-ITC-SDWR-SpeakingToTheDeadWithRadios-/?yguid=338683728

Or through facebook® at The Worldwide Radio Sweep - Ghost Box EVP Alliance at this URL http://www.facebook.com/groups/102193593178906/